THE ILLUSTRATED GUIDE TO
ASTROLOGY

The Key to Understanding
Human Destiny

THE ILLUSTRATED GUIDE TO
ASTROLOGY

The Key to Understanding
Human Destiny

Edited by

T. Wynne Griffon

MALLARD
PRESS

ACKNOWLEDGEMENTS

Without the pioneering work of the great scholars Manley Palmer Hall and Nicholas DeVore, this work would not have been possible. The writings of Walter B Gibson and Litzka R Gibson were also profoundly integral to the present work.

Page 1: A Medieval woodcut of the 12 signs of the Zodiac as they wheel, with the sun and moon, around an Earthly kingdom.
Pages 2–3: The constellation Sagittarius, in which the experienced eye can pick out the shape of the Sagittarius the archer.
These pages: Woodcuts from the *Poeticon Astronomicon* by Hyginus (cut in Venice in 1482).

TABLE OF CONTENTS

INTRODUCTION

As the great scholar Manly Palmer Hall wrote in 1933, 'The proper end of all learning is to discover Cause. Science exists that it may glorify fact and establish truth, yet for certain reasons entirely beyond scientific control, Cause remains unknown, fact is obscure, and truth only a word. The layman, seeking knowledge of the sidereal world, naturally turns to the astronomer whose self-appointed task it is to measure the immensities of space and classify the great energies that are resident therein.'

If the modern astronomer solemnly announces that the heavenly bodies can produce no moral effect upon the Earth, this pronouncement is regarded as scriptural in its finality. It seldom occurs to the average person that the astronomer has *proved* nothing by his solemn pronouncement and, if the truth were known, is not in a position to prove anything. Astrology has never been scientifically disproved—all blustering to the contrary notwithstanding.

The great Sir Issac Newton, who combined excellence of intellect with a becoming humility, was brought to the study of astronomy by his early interest in astrology. On one occasion, when complimented upon the profundity of his erudition, Newton replied with a gentle smile, 'If I appear to see farther than other men, it is because I am standing upon the shoulders of giants.' We would humbly remind the modern scientist that he, too, is greatly indebted to the ages for that wisdom which is now his boast. The giants upon whose shoulders Newton stood were Pythagoras, Ptolemy, Copernicus, Galileo, Kepler and Brahe. These illustrious men were all astrologers but showed none of the symptoms of that mental deterioration from which, according to modern science, all astrologers suffer.

It is, therefore, far from scientific heresy to suggest that a subject, which has occupied the minds of the world's ablest thinkers for the entire period of the world's recorded history, might be worthy of a more tolerant attitude by today's critics.

At left: **The brighter stars in this view are the seven Pleiades, who serve as the nose ring for the constellation Taurus, the bull.**

Astrology is a well-founded tradition, thoroughly established in the three great requisites of knowledge—authority, observation and experimentation—which, according to Sir Francis Bacon, are the proper bases for the building up of a scientific premise. Writing in *De Augmentis*, he states definitely that astrology may be 'more confidently' applied to prophecy: 'Predictions may be made of comets to come, which (I am inclined to think) may be foretold; of all kinds of meteors, of floods, droughts, heats, frosts, earthquakes, eruptions of water, eruptions of fire, great winds and rains, various seasons of the year, plagues, epidemic diseases, plenty and dearth of grain, wars, sedition, schisms, transmigrations of peoples and any other or all commotions or general revolutions of things, natural as well as civil.'

Modern astronomy deals only with the physical composition of the cosmos. Ancient astronomers—the astrologers—were concerned primarily with the intellectual and moral *energy* of the universe. Materialism in the twentieth century has perverted the application of knowledge from its legitimate ends, thus permitting so noble a science as astronomy to become a purely abstract, and comparatively useless, instrument which can contribute little more than tables of meaningless figures to a world bankrupt in spiritual, philosophical and ethical values. In Manly Palmer Hall's day a half century ago, the public was assured that the old science was practically defunct, and leading educators glossed over the whole matter by referring to astrology as extinct.

The fact is that astrology *today* has a greater number of advocates than ever before in its long and illustrious history. Bookstores and librarians will testify that works on this subject are in ever-increasing demand and the standard of their scholarship is constantly improving.

The twelve signs of the zodiac are the basic building blocks, not only of astrology, but of all human destiny. Their organization within the zodiac is the key to the art and science of astrology, while the *nature* of the twelve signs is the key to understanding the nature of human existence and our place within the cosmos!

Again, to quote Manly Palmer Hall from 1933, 'The case rests upon the facts.'

THE HISTORY OF ASTROLOGY

The science of the stars has not been established merely upon dogma and belief, but derives it authority from thousands of years of observation by those who Manley Palmer Hall describes as 'philosophers of the highest refinement.' Astrology was practiced by the earliest civilized peoples of the Earth, and in every period of philosophic and spiritual enlightenment was accorded a place of honor by those of high birth and great learning.

In his first book, *Divination*, Cicero observed that the Chaldeans had records of the stars for the space of 370,000 years; Diodorus Siculus calculated that their observations comprehended the space of 473,000 years. Cicero further maintains that the Babylonians, over a period of many thousands of years, kept the nativities (horoscopes) of all children who were born among them, and from this enormous mass of data circulated the effects of the various planets and zodiacal signs.

'The Sumerians and Babylonians believed,' wrote noted Middle East scholar Sir EA Wallis-Budge, 'that the will of the gods in respect to man and his affairs could be learned by watching the motions of the stars and planets, and that skilled stargazers could obtain from the motions and varying aspects of the heavenly

In Medieval times, Christian cosmology was architecturally expressed in such as this thirteenth-century cathedral *(at left)* in Brabant. Astrology was kept alive by clerics whose interests took a slightly liberal turn.

bodies indications of future prosperity and calamity. They therefore caused observations to be made and recorded on tablets, which they interpreted from a magical, and not astronomical, point of view, and these observations and their comments on them, and interpretation of them, have formed the foundation of the astrology that has been in use for the last 5000 years. According to ancient traditions preserved by Greek writers, the Babylonians made these observations for some hundreds of thousands of years, and though we must reject such fabulous statements, we are bound to believe that the period during which observations of the heavens were made on the plains of Babylonia comprised many thousands of years.'

The earliest Egyptian astrologers to be mentioned in manuscripts were the nobleman Petosiris and the priest Necepso, who lived at approximately the time of Rameses II. Reference is made to these 'astromancers' in the writings of Atheraeus, Aristophanes, Juvenal, Pliny, Galen, Ptolemy and Suidas. From the testimony of these authors, there can be little doubt that both Petosiris and Necepso left extensive writings on astrological subjects, although little has been preserved to this age. Even during the period of the later Greek writers these two men were looked upon as semidivine personages who had received their knowledge directly from Hermes and Asclepius.

According to Albert Pike, the distinguished Masonic scholar, books on astrology were carried with the deepest reverence in the religious processionals of the Egyptians. The astrologers of Oxydraces came to Alexander the Great when he invaded India and explained to him certain of the secrets of the heavenly science. The Brahmans, whom Apollonius of Tyana visited in the first century of the Christian era, were also deeply learned in the mysteries of the stars. In China, astrology set forth the rules by which both the state and the family were to be governed. The Arabians deemed it the mother of sciences. The Roman astrologer Valens drew up, by royal command, the horoscope of Constantine the Great.

After noting that the great Hermes, Ptolemy, King of Egypt and Zoroaster, the first of the Magi, were patrons of astrology and had examined carefully into its mysteries, Her Royal Highness, Princess of Cumberland, wrote: 'How ignorant and prejudiced, then, must that man be, and how crude with understanding, which condemns a science in which the wisest and greatest king of the Earth, even Solomon, delighted.'

The original 'Raphael' (RC Smith), who styled himself 'the astrologer of the nineteenth century,' declared that in former times astrology was comparable to a mighty colossus that overstrode all other sciences, and that even in this incredulous era it has 'enlightened the gloomy atmosphere of unbelief by some remarkable prediction. Astrology has well been denominated the 'rule of kings, and, by virtue of the excellence of the art itself, has survived the crash of empires, the vicissitudes of ages and the revolutions of public opinion.'

The Egyptians maintained that the sciences of astrology and alchemy were bestowed upon man by the benevolence of the gods. The elder nations of the Earth conceded the Egyptian premise, but each claimed that its own philosophers were the first to cultivate the 'imperishable art.'

Astrology was practiced in India thousands of years before the compiling of the Vedas. The great magician and astrologer Asuramaya was born in Atlantis, thus testifying upon the authority of the *Puranas* to the extreme antiquity of the celestial science.

The oldest traditions of China are concerned, among other things, with the qualities and attributes of the five planetary emperors of the world and the dynasty of starry kings that preceded human rulers.

Josephus, speaking for the Jews, affirms that Adam was instructed in astrology by heavenly inspiration. According to Diodorus, Hercules was accredited with having revealed the art to the Greeks, but this is probably an allegorical allusion to the Sun.

Lucian, however, held that Orpheus brought the principles of astrology from India, and that 'the planets were signified by the seven strings of his lyre.'

Indeed, there is no corner of the Earth where those who are the wisest of their race and time have not read and pondered what James Gaffarel, astrologer to Cardinal Richelieu, so wisely termed 'the handwriting on the wall of heaven.'

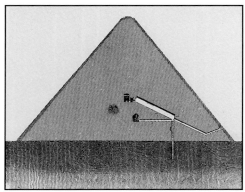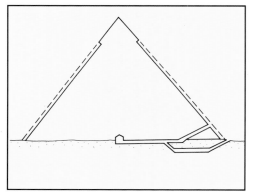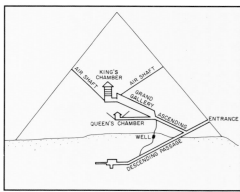

At top, above: **The Egyptian pyramids at Giza. Seen here are the pyramids of Sneferu and Khefren, and the Great Pyramid of Cheops. The ancient Egyptians practiced astrology, and the pyramids are felt by some to have profound astrological significance. Scientists are enthralled, for as they study the architecture of these 2000–3000-year-old royal tombs, they feel it is in some way possible to comprehend the minds that built them. As can be seen by the cutaway view *above left*, Cheops's Pyramid contained the tomb chambers of the Pharaoh himself.**

Mysterious passageways connect the tomb chambers with deliberate traps to foil tomb robbers. An inexplicable departure from this motif are the passageways and tomb chamber of the pyramid of Khefren (*above, center*). The tomb chamber is not the royal tomb chamber of Pharaoh Khefren, and the passageways lead directly to the outside. Indeed, after extensive scientific investigation, Khefren's tomb seems to be nowhere in the pyramid: was it then built as an astronomical observatory? Contrast this with the Great Pyramid of Cheops (*above right*), built by Khefren's father. This complex arrangement of passageways is felt by some to embody a coded 'message for the ages.'

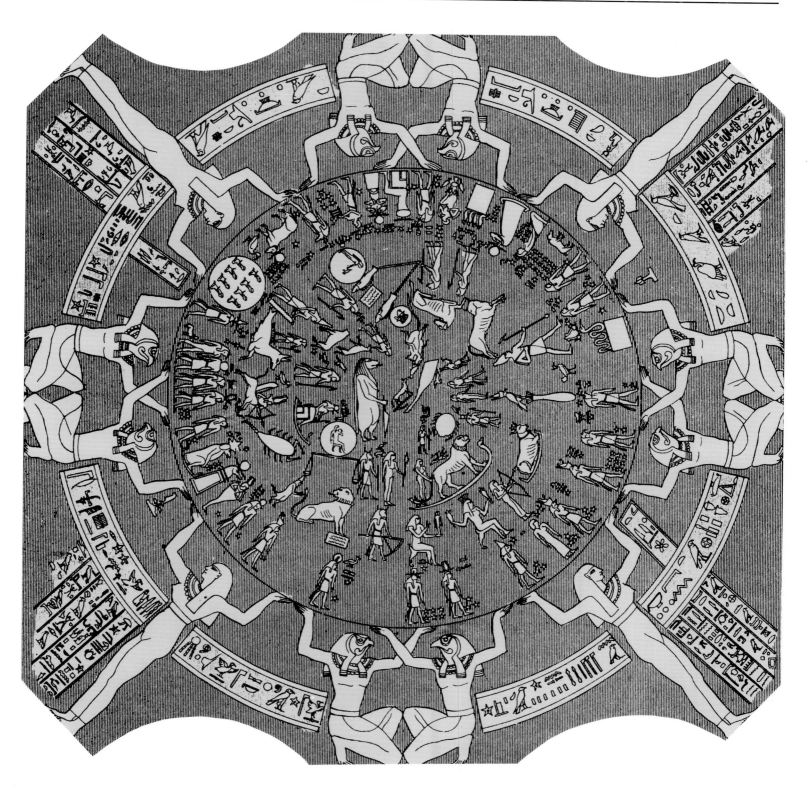

Above: The ceiling from the temple of Hathor at Dendera in Upper Egypt. This Egyptian zodiac dates back to 30 BC. Astrology was imported to Egypt from still older cultures, and with its reputation of forecasting the future, it soon became popular with those in positions of power. The Zodiac (as it is portrayed even *to this day*) is discernable in the psychic creatures of the Egyptian pantheon that are here portrayed.

At the top of the innermost ring of figures is Pisces, the fish; and going counter-clockwise from Pisces, we find Aquarius, the water carrier; Capricorn, the sea-goat; Sagittarius, the archer; Scorpio, the scorpion; Libra, the scales; Virgo, the virgin; Leo, the lion; Cancer, the crab (in Egypt represented as a scarab beetle); Gemini, the twins (here seen as a man and a woman with joined hands); Taurus, the bull; and Aries, the ram.

The planets are also shown here, and their symbols appear with the sign in which they were felt to have the most influence. Thus, we find Venus in Pisces; Mars in Capricorn; Mercury in Virgo; Saturn in Libra; and Jupiter in Cancer. The outer wheel is interpreted as indicating the precession of the equinoxes: ostensibly, the Egyptians arrived at their non-mathematical system by allegorical means, which would have required sharp observation.

WESTERN TRADITIONS

There have been many illustrious exponents of astrology, both ancient and modern. In fact, few branches of learning have been more adequately represented or have won better patronage. Of the famous personages of the last few centuries addicted to the study of astrology, many must remain unknown. For, as Professor Max Mueller, the great Orientalist, has noted, while many of the greatest intellects have studied astrology, the majority have never expressed their opinions on the subject for fear of public criticism.

In an article on astrology in the writings of Shakespeare, John Cook thus summarizes the results of an extensive research: 'The numerous allusions to the practice of astrology, the striking metaphors and apt illustrations, scattered throughout the plays of Shakespeare, at once attest to his intimate acquaintance with the general principles of the science, and the popularity of astrological faith…. He has left us sufficient evidence to show that he was largely influenced by a subject which has left indelible marks in the language and literature of England.'

The bard of Avon puts the following words into the mouth of King Lear: 'It is the stars, the stars above us govern our conditions.'

Even more striking is his flair for astrologic humor. He makes a disgruntled player to complain: 'It is impossible that anything should be as I would have it; for I was born, Sir, when the Crab was ascending; and all my affairs go backwards.'

Dante's astrology is written in majestic measure. We follow him into the vastness of space in his *Paradiso* (Canto XXII):

'…I saw
The sign that follows Taurus, and was in it.
Oh glorious stars! Oh light impregnated
With mighty virtues, from which I acknowledge
All of my genius whatsoe'er it be,
With you was born, and hid himself with you.
He who is father of all mortal life,
When first I tasted of the Tuscan air;
And then when grace was freely given to me
To enter the high wheel which turns you round
Your region was alloted unto me.'

'For Dante, astrology was the noblest of the sciences,' writes H Flanders Dunbar in *Symbolism in Medieval Thought*. 'For Dante, the principle of individualization is the influence of planets and stars, or, more accurately, of the intelligences by which they are moved. The ego, created directly by God, in its connection with the body comes under stellar influence, and at birth is stamped like wax by a seal. All impressions from the stars are good, since there is no lovableness that does not reflect the lovableness of God. It is the harmonizing and proportioning of these good qualities in their true relationships that make this or that person more or less perfect. It is likely that the modern reader, with his oversimple conception of astrology, will lose much of the meaning of Dante… Astrology was both more complicated and more scientific in method than the familiar birth-month pamphlets suggest.'

Goethe commits himself in no uncertain terms to both the theory and practice of astrology. He begins his autobiography thus: 'On the 28th of August 1749, at midday, as the clock struck twelve, I came into the world, at Frankfurt-on-Main. The aspect of the stars was propitious: the Sun stood in the sign of the Virgin, and had culminated for the day; Jupiter and Venus looked on with a friendly eye, and Mercury not adversely; the attitude of Saturn and

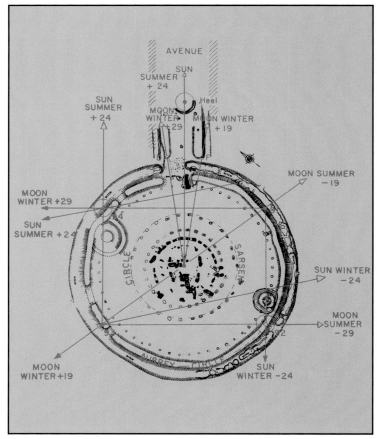

Above: An overhead view of Stonehenge, on England's Salisbury Plain—a 2000-year-old solar and lunar observatory, laid out as a 328-foot-in-diameter (measured from the outer circle) astrolabe. Astronomer Gerald Hawkins established the existence of numerous solstice—and lunar standstill—alignments, which are shown here.

At top, above: A metaphysical seeker encounters a new realm of knowledge. This woodcut is popularly thought to date from the fifteenth or sixteenth century, but was probably the handiwork of the nineteenth-century Frenchman, Camille Flammarion, an advocate of astrology.

At right: In order of their nearness to the current conception, these are cosmological models as conceived by Ptolemy (second century AD); Plato (428–348 BC); the ancient Egyptians; Tycho Brahe (1546–1601); an unnamed disciple of Tycho; and Nicholas Copernicus (1473–1543). Only in the Copernican model is the Sun the center of the cosmos.

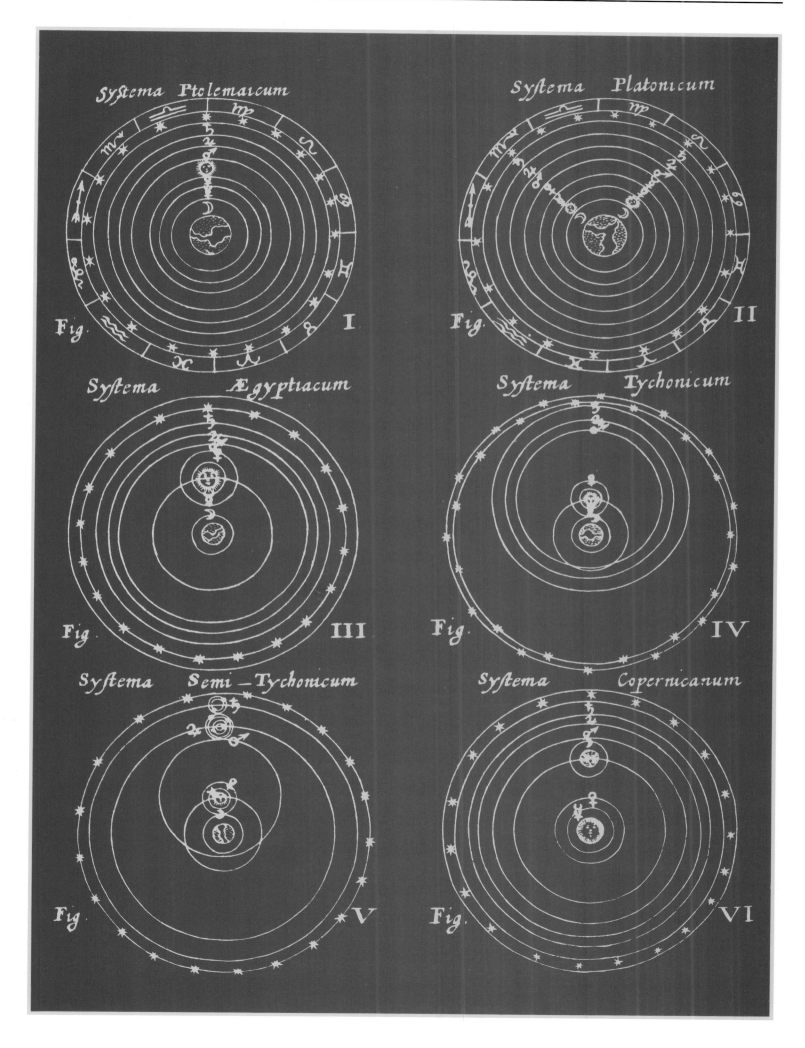

Mars was neutral; the Moon alone, just full, exerted all the more influence as her power of opposition had just reached her planetary hour. She, therefore, resisted my birth, which could not be accomplished until this hour was passed. These auspicious aspects which the astrologers subsequently interpreted very favorably for me may have been the causes of my preservation.'

'Do not Christians and heathens, Jews and gentiles, poets and philosophers,' writes Sir Walter Scott, 'unite in allowing the starry influences?'

Nor is science represented by less impressive names. According to Thorndike in his *History of Magic and Experimental Science*, 'A trio of great names, Pliny, Galen and Ptolemy, stand out above all others in the history of science in the Roman Empire.' Needless to say, all these distinguished thinkers not only admitted the influence of the planets upon human life but wrote at some length on the science of astrology.

The names of other astrologer-scientists are certainly no less renowned; Hippocrates, the father of medicine; Vitruvius, the master of architecture; Placidus, the mathematician; Giordan Bruno, the martyr; Jerome Cardan, the mathematician; and Copernicus. In *Galileo*, Emile Namer wrote that 'Galileo himself, father of modern science, read his children's horoscopes at their births.'

Tycho Brahe, Regiomontanus, Kepler, Huygens and Flammarion, the astronomers; Roger Bacon, the Benedictine monk; Sir Francis Bacon, the father of modern science; Baron Napier, of Merchistoun, the inventor of logarithms; Flamsteed, the first astronomer royal and founder of Greenwich Observatory; Sir Elias Ashmole, the founder of the Ashmolean Museum at Oxford; and Sir Christopher Heydon, who wrote a lengthy treatise in defense of judicial astrology.

'In the traditions of astrology,' wrote Sir Francis Bacon, 'the natures and dispositions of men are not without truth distinguished from the predominances of the planets.'

Tycho Brahe declares, 'The stars rule the lot of man.'

Although Sir Issac Newton is not generally considered a defender of astrology, he was led to the study of astronomy by the interest aroused through the reading of astrological books. It is recorded that when the astronomer Sir Edmund Halley, of comet fame, made a slighting remark as to the value of astrology, Newton gently rebuked him thus: 'I have studied the subject, Mr Halley; you have not.'

At this point it is appropriate to insert three well authenticated accounts of astrological prediction. The high integrity of the authorities involved demands a respectful consideration of their statements. The Archbishop of St Andrews, having a disease which baffled the physicians of England, sent to the Continent in 1552, begging assistance of the mathematician-astrologer Jerome Cardan. After erecting the horoscope of the prelate by which the disease was discovered and cured, Cardan took his leave in these words: 'I have been able to cure you of your sickness, but cannot change your destiny, nor prevent you from being hung.' Eighteen years later this churchman was hung by order of the commissioners appointed by Mary, Queen of Scots. As he was passing through the city of London on his return home, Cardan was also engaged to calculate the nativity of King Edward VI.

The second example relates to a celebrated prophecy by the noted astronomer Tycho Brahe. From a study of the great comet of 1577, Brahe was led to declare that, 'In the north, in Finland, there should be born a prince who should lay waste Germany and vanish in 1632.' Time proved the accuracy of the comet's warning. The prince, Gustavus Adolphus, was born in Finland, ravaged Germany during the Thirty Years' War, and died as the astronomer had predicted in 1632. The *Encyclopedia Britannica* comments thus upon the circumstance: 'The fulfillment of the details of this

Above far left: Tycho Brahe (1546–1601), the Danish astronomer, was an active astrologer as well. He declared, 'The stars rule the lot of man.'

At far left: Tycho Brahe's early plans for a giant astrolabe—an 'update' of Stonehenge, so to speak. The astrolabe was a device for determining the positions of stars, and therefore was of critical importance to practitioners of both astronomy *and* astrology.

Above left: Nicholas Copernicus (1473–1543), the Polish astronomer who is known as the founder of modern astronomy, was among the many men of science who studied astrology.

At left: Galileo Galilei (1564–1642), the first notable astronomer to use a telescope, believed in the practice of astrology. Galileo is also responsible for the discovery, in December 1609 and January 1610, of the four larger moons of Jupiter, which he named Io, Europa, Ganymede and Callisto. Upon doing so, he became the first man since the ancients to name celestial bodies in our Solar System.

Above: The Leaning Tower of Pisa, built as a bell tower for the Cathedral of Pisa: its pronounced tilt is caused by the tower's settling in the sandy foundation soil. It was sometimes used by Galileo as an observatory, and for determining the velocities of falling objects. It was also from this great landmark that he observed Jupiter's moons.

prophecy suggests that Tycho Brahe had some basis of reason for his prediction.'

The third account is taken from Lord Bacon's *Essay on Prophecy*. He writes: 'When I was in France, I heard from one Doctor Pena, that the Queen Mother, who was given to curious arts, caused the king, her husband's, nativity to be calculated under a false name; and the astrologer gave a judgment that he would be killed in a duel; at which the Queen laughed, thinking her husband to be above challenges and duels; but was slain, upon a course at tilt, the splinters of the staffe of Montgomery going in at his bever.'

St Augustine admitted the accuracy of astrology, but attributed the science to infernal agencies. Albertus Magnus, beatified bishop and architect, and his disciple, the great St Thomas Aquinas (one of the most learned of medieval divines), both acknowledged the power of the planets over mundane affairs. 'All that Nature and art produces,' wrote Albertus Magnus, 'is driven by celestial powers.' And St Thomas Aquinas adds: 'The celestial bodies are the cause of all that takes place in this sublunar world.'

Other great Western astrologers included Melanchthon, the Rev Dr Butler, 'Protestant Minister of the True, Ancient, Catholick and Apostolik Faith of the Church of England,' as well as Jacob Boehme, the seer of Seidenburg, not to mention His Eminence, the Cardinal, Duc de Richelieu, and the great Jesuit scholar Athanasius Kircher.

The Holy See can boast of several astrologer-popes, including Sylvester, John XX, John XXI, Sixtus IV, Julius II, Alexander IV, Leo X, Paul III, Clement VII and Calixtus III. According to Temple Hungad, Maresilio Ficino, the astrologer to the household of Lorenzo the Magnificent, casting the horoscopes of the children of that illustrious de Medici, predicted that little Giovanni was destined to become a pope. When, later, this occurred and he ascended to the holy chair as Pope Leo X, he became a distinguished patron of astrology and a great believer in the ancient science. Pope Julius II had the day of his coronation set by astrology, while Sixtus IV arranged his audiences according to planetary hours. It is said of Paul III that he never held a consistory except when the heavenly bodies were propitious.

The four greatest conquerors of historic times—Alexander the Great, Julius Caesar, Genghis Khan and Napoleon I—devoutly believed in the 'heavenly' government of the world.

The Brahman sages revealed to Alexander not only the time of his death but the manner thereof—that he should perish from a cup. When Alexander reached the walls of Babylon the astrologers warned him away, saying 'Flee from this town where thy fatal star reigns.' Alexander was deeply impressed by this warning and for a time turned aside from Babylon. Later he entered the city where he came by his death.

According to Lucian, Caesar noted the revolutions of the stars in the midst of his preparations for battle. The mathematician Spurina warned the immortal Julius that his Mars threatened violence during the Ides of March, and the outcome of this latter admonition is, as they say, history.

Genghis Khan appointed astrologers to positions of honor in his suite, and one of them, Ye Liu Chutsai, was his constant advisor during Khan's victorious march across half the world.

Napoleon pointed out his guiding star to Cardinal Fesch, his uncle, but that worthy churchman had not the vision to perceive it. The first Emperor of the French put such faith in the 'testimony of the suns' that he frequently sought the advice of the celebrated French seeress Mademoiselle Le Normand. In justice to the ability of this remarkable woman, it should be remembered that she warned him repeatedly *against* a Russian campaign.

Napoleon's fall was largely due to a futile attempt to outwit his Saturn, which raised him up only to cast him down. 'Wallenstein was in his tower consulting the portents of fate. Josephine was ex-tending her hand not yet imperial, to the sable fortune-teller; while Napoleon, trusting to the star of his destiny, was following it from victory to victory and from triumph to triumph till it burst forth as "the Sun of Austerlitz". These and examples like these, exercise a strange fascination over the feelings which is not wholly due to the magnitude of the interests or the eminence of the personages with which such fancies are entwined.'

Sir Henry Cornelius Agrippa was astrologer to Charles I of France, but lost that office because of the consistent manner in which he predicted misfortune. King Charles VII of France is said to have attended classes in astrology.

Catherine de Medici was profoundly versed in the heavenly lore and was the patroness of Nostradamus, the most famous of the French astrologers and physician to King Henry II and Charles IX. The prophecies of Nostradamus, 'set forth in a pamphlet, were read all over the world. Although he died in 1566, his forebodings were believed in as late as the eighteenth century, for at its beginning a Papal Edict forbade the sale of the booklet, as it proclaimed the downfall of the Papacy.' He also prophesied the great fire of London in 1666, the French Revolution and the advent of Napoleon centuries before these circumstances took place, and in the case of Napoleon gave a very accurate description of his person and temperament. Nostradamus' prediction of the London fire is as follows:

'The blood o' th' just requires,
Which out of London reeks,
That it be raz'd with fires,
in year threescore and six.'

Nostradamus also predicted the rise and fall of the Third Reich (1933-1945) and the assassinations of the Kennedy brothers (1963 and 1968).

Louis XI consulted the astrologers Angelo Catto and d'Almonsor and maintained in royal style the celebrated astrologer Baleotti Martius. The latter is described by Sir Walter Scott in these glowing terms:

'Martius was none of those ascetic, withered, pale professors of mystic learning of those days, who bleared their eyes over the midnight furnace, and macerated their bodies by out-matching the polar bear. He was trained in arms and renowned as a wrestler. His apartment was splendidly furnished, and on a large oaken table lay a variety of mathematical and astrological instruments, all of the most rich materials and curious workmanship. His astrolabe of silver was the gift of the Emperor of Germany, and his Jacob's staff of ebony jointed with gold was a mark of esteem from the reigning pope. In person, the astrologer was a tall, bulky, yet stately man. His features, though rather overgrown, were dignified and noble, and a Samson might have envied the dark, downward sweep of his long descending beard. His dress was a chamber-robe of the richest Genoa velvet, with ample sleeves clasped with frogs of gold and lined with sables. It was fastened round his middle by a broad belt of virgin parchment, round which were represented in crimson characters the signs of the zodiac.'

A planetary conjunction in Pisces, long predicted for 1524, spawned fears of global calamities, and inspired Hieronymous Bosch (1450–1516) to paint the scene *at above right*, in 1498. Here we see the ascetic hermit St Anthony of Coma assaulted by screeching demons, many of whom have assumed the fishlike, Piscean form.

At right: **A depiction of apocalyptic despair by Peter Brueghel (1525–1569). Time, devourer of youth, lords the infinite 'Snake Uroboros' over a benighted Earth, which is dragged through a blasted landscape by the weary Horses of the Sun, as the signs of the Zodiac continue their work.**

Benjamin Franklin, the great American scientist, philosopher, diplomat, and the founder of the *Saturday Evening Post*, published a series of almanacs under the pseudonym of Richard Saunders, or Poor Richard. He borrowed this name from a distinguished astrologer-physician of the preceding century, whose great textbook on medical astrology, published in 1677, contained an introduction by the most celebrated of the English astrologers, William Lilly. America's first Ambassador to France did not hesitate to acknowledge that he communed with the Uranian Muse. In comparing this notable Philadelphian with some of our more recent politicians, Manly Palmer Hall wonders whether it would 'not be wise to make astrology compulsory for diplomats.'

Theodore Roosevelt, twenty-sixth president of the United States, whose smile made a multitude of friends and whose 'big stick' made political history, seems to have had more than a passing interest in the stars — especially his own stars. In this regard we quote three paragraphs from an article, *Roosevelt and Astro-Science*, by Janice C Hunter:

'Mr Dudley Clarke, traveler and author of many books on Masonic and Biblical symbolism, informed the writer that he had known President Roosevelt personally, and had discussed his birth-chart with him upon several occasions. Mr Clarke stated that the President had informed him that his father was a believer in the ancient science to the extent that he had the horoscope of the future president of the United States constructed by the father of Li Hung Chang, the Chinese statesman and general, when his young son and heir was just ten hours old.

'Upon one occasion when Mr Clarke reminded President Roosevelt that he had some rather disconcerting squares in his chart, the President laughingly waved these aside with the remark that he intended to live by his sextile and trine. Even then, however, to his oft-voiced principle in later years, viz: "Trust God, but keep your powder dry." The President confided to Mr Clarke that he always kept his weather-eye on the opposition of the Moon in his seventh house to Mars in his first.

'Mr Clarke stated that Roosevelt himself enlarged and etched his natal figure on some durable material, and had mounted it on a chessboard which always stood on a table in his room, and that when Roosevelt was contemplating some momentous undertaking, he would estimate the facility with which it would be accomplished, or the difficulties attending its consummation, by his ability to quickly checkmate the Queen, which represented the Moon opposing Mars in his horoscope.'

An outstanding exponent of astrology in early twentieth century America was the late Evageline Adams, a descendant of John Quincy Adams, sixth president of the United States. Ms Adams successfully defended astrology before the courts in 1932, and at the end of the case the judge said, 'The defendant raises astrology to the dignity of an exact science. Every fortuneteller is a violator of the law, but every astrologer is not a fortuneteller.'

The humble and the great flocked to Ms Adams' studios in Carnegie Hall in New York City. King Edward VII, Enrico Caruso, John Burroughs, Geraldine Farrar and Mary Pickford were among her clients. To quote the *New York World* of 11 November 1932, 'Businessmen came too; even J Pierpont Morgan (Sr) and two former presidents of the New York Stock Exchange, Seymour Cromwell and Jacob Stout. "I read Mr Morgan's horoscope many times," Ms Adams said. "He was skeptical at first. But I convinced him. During the last years of his life I furnished him a regular service. It explained the general effects of the planets on politics, business and the stock market." '

Adolf Hitler, born under the sign of Taurus on 20 April 1889, was a believer in astrology, as were many other persons of high position within the German Reich between 1933 and 1945. The British

Foreign Secretary Lord Halifax was also a believer, and in 1940 he hired Hitler's former astrologer Ludwig von Wohl as a consultant on Hitler's horoscope.

According to von Wohl, Adolf Hitler had first consulted the astrologer Baron Rudolf Freihern von Sebottendorf in 1923. The Baron, whose real name was Adam Glandeck, advised Hitler *not* to undertake anything of importance during November of that year, but Hitler ignored him. When the famous 'Beer Hall Putsch' of 8 November 1923 failed and Hitler found himself in jail, he became a believer.

During the first years of World War II, one of the major astrologers in the service of the Reich was Karl Ernst Krafft, who was a psychological consultant to Heinrich Himmler's Office for State Security. One of Krafft's predictions is credited with saving the Fuhrer from an assassination attempt in November 1939. However, this did not spare Krafft from arrest in June 1941 on the orders of Rudolf Hess as part of a general official campaign against astrology. Nonetheless, many astrologers, including Krafft and the mysterious Dr Wulff of Hamburg, continued to serve the aims of Germany's war effort.

During April 1945 when the Nazi empire was on the verge of collapse, Hitler had two horoscopes done — his own and that of the Reich itself. They suggested victory would be snatched from the jaws of defeat in the same way as it had been for Frederick the Great at the end of the Seven Years War. The death of President Franklin D Roosevelt a few days later was seen as auspicious, but

Hitler was nonetheless doomed. It seems that his astrologers had given him false data in order to save their own lives.

Many, indeed most, great world leaders have been followers of the stars. In May 1988, for example, it was revealed that President Ronald Reagan and his wife Nancy were firm believers. Through the well known San Francisco astrologer Joan Quigley, Mr and Mrs Reagan used the stars to guide their highly successful eight-year tenure in the White House. Ms Quigley predicted that late March 1981 would be dangerous for the president. Thus, after the 30 March assassination attempt during which Mr Reagan was severely wounded, presidential appearances were no longer scheduled without first consulting Ms Quigley. This meant a several-hour delay for the start of Mr Reagan's 1984 trip to Europe, but success for the trip itself.

In 1987 Ms Quigley was consulted to pick the precise hour for the signing of the historic treaty with the Soviet Union which limited the number of intermediate nuclear weapons in Europe. She accomplished this by casting the horoscopes of both President Reagan (Aquarius) and Soviet Premier Mikhail Gorbachev (Pisces).

Above far left: **Adolf Hitler, a Taurus on the Aries cusp with Leo in the tenth house and Libra ascending, was born on 20 April 1889. Venus conjuncts with Mars in his seventh house (attitude toward other nations). Saturn in the tenth (Uranus and Mercury in the ninth) portend warlike attitudes. Hitler abandoned restraint, and his tendencies led to World War II.**

Above: **Former US President Ronald Reagan (6 February 1911), an Aquarius, was said to schedule trips during his White House years using Joan Quigley horoscopes.**

Tortured as a sorcerer in one era, ridiculed as a charlatan in another and raised to highest honors in more generous times, the astrologer has survived the numerous 'physical changes in the moral and intellectual world.'

Like the fabled phoenix, astrology has risen again and again victoriously from its own ashes. Vilified and traduced by the sophists of every age, but vindicated and evidenced by Nature herself, astrology still gathers luster from its own stars, and now in the twentieth century it may truthfully be said that the whole civilized world is astrology conscious.

THE FAR EAST

According to Richard Allen, the ancient Chinese ascribed the formation of constellations to Ta Jao, the Prime Minister to Emperor Hwang Ti, and made much of an observation of the Pleiades in 2537 BC, from an observatory said to have been erected in 2608 BC. Analysis of Chinese thought gravitates decidedly against the popular belief that the Chinese derived their astrology from the Arabs or the Hindus.

In 1931 in his *Splendour of the Heavens*, TER Phillips, the Honorable Secretary of the Royal Astronomical Society, wrote, 'The ancient Chinese zodiac is quite independent of that in use in the West. It is clear that China was one of the leading nations of antiquity in astronomical study.'

It is true that modern Chinese astrology was profoundly influenced by later contact with European civilization, but it is also true that the latter culture is utterly distinct from the older learning. The modifications of early systems and the new interpretations given to ancient doctrines, which resulted from the introduction of Jesuitism in Cathay, should not deceive the critical investigator nor lead him to depreciate the profound significance of the indigenous arts, traditions and sciences. Gaubil summarizes the opinions of Jesuit scholars to the effect that the Chinese presumed the relationships existing between terrestrial rulers and their subjects to be controlled by the motions and positions of celestial bodies and other sidereal phenomena. It was to discover these relationships that the Chinese astronomers of all ages primarily directed their efforts.

AJ Pearce writes further that 'astrology was firmly established among the learned Chinese from the earliest periods in the history of their remarkable country from the days of Fohi, about 2752 years BC.'

Confucius is unquestionably the outstanding ethical force in China. Although he admitted his inability to comprehend the metaphysical abstractions of Lao-tse, he was nevertheless a man of profound mentality, with a firm grasp upon the practical issues of life. His birth was announced by a strange vision in which five ancient and mysterious sages appeared, leading in their midst a lion-like creature covered with the scales of a dragon and carrying a short horn in the middle of its forehead. This annunciation is susceptible of an astrological rendering. The dragon-lion of China, like the phoenix of Arabia and Egypt, signifies a certain time cycle, and at the climax of each cycle the heavens produce a 'superior man.' The five ancient sages, like the five sidereal emperors, were the planets, which added further testimony to that of the cycle, for they are spoken of as bringing in, or leading, the sacred animal.

The astrology of the ancient Chinese is established upon the line of imperial descent, for under the old regime the emperor was the Son of Heaven, the direct descendant of the azure God of the Sky. Among the most important ceremonials of the empire was the annual celebration of the happy new year, which took place on the night of the winter solstice, when Yang, the Spirit of Light, began to increase. South of Peking there is an altar of heaven in the midst of an imaginary well made up of the philosophic diagrams of Fohi. The altar is circular in shape and rises in three tiers, each level being surrounded by a carved marble balustrade. Upon the night of the winter solstice the whole area in which the altar stands was weirdly lighted by torches. On the upper terrace, or altar proper, there stood a tablet bearing the inscription, 'Imperial Heaven, Supreme Emperor.'

There were also rows of similar tablets dedicated to emperors of the divine line who have intervened between the first divine

Above: A chart of the Hindu Zodiac. The Hindus claim to be the oldest surviving culture in continuous use of astrology. *At right:* A Tibetan mandala. The Tibetans use fixed cycles—not an ephemeris—in astrology.

emperor and his then worshipping descendant. Upon the second terrace were tablets to the Sun, the Moon, the five planets, the Great Bear, the 28 principal constellations (lunar mansions) and the other important stars of heaven. The princes of the realm, the great mandarins, and other dignitaries all stood in their appointed places during the ceremony. When everything was in readiness, the emperor ascended into the presence of the tablet of 'High Heaven' and, bowing humbly before the venerable past, knelt and knocked his forehead against the marble pavement, beseeching the Great Emperor above to look with favor upon his earthly son and to protect the empire.

Tibetan astrologers, meanwhile, do not make use of an ephemeris, their calculations being from fixed cycles rather than from actual planetary positions. Strangely enough, their system is amazingly accurate, and their method—the secret of which they still zealously guard—compares favorably in the matter of results with the more complicated Brahmanic and Ptolemaic schools.

On the Indian subcontinent, an examination of the Vedas, Puranas and other religio-historical documents of the ancient Aryans seems to fully justify the claim for the priority of Hindu astrology as advanced by V Subrahmanya Sas'tri. In the preface to his translation of the *Brihat Jataka*, Mr Sastri makes the unqualified statement that 'the Hindus are the oldest surviving nation in the world and astrology is their oldest science.' Sir William Jones, the distinguised Orientalist, defends the antiquity of the Hindu zodiac against the prevailing opinions of Western scholars that it had been derived later from the learning of foreign nations. 'In the first place,' Jones declares in his *The Science of Foreknowledge*, 'the Brahmans were always too proud to borrow their science from the Greeks, Arabs, Mongols or any nation of Mlechchhas (as they call those who are ignorant of the Vedas and have not studied the language of the Gods).'

Dr VG Rele is also convinced that the astrology of the Hindus is indigenous. 'That the antiquity of the Indian astrology,' he notes in his *An Exposition of the Directional Astrology of the Hindus*, 'is as remote as the Vedas, is a fact which is not difficult to prove. It

forms one of the Angas of the *Atharva-Veda*.' After observing that the *Jyotish Shastra*, a work devoted to the movements of the celestial bodies and their significance, is mentioned in the *Atharva-Veda*, he concludes: 'It will thus be seen that the origin of the present astrology is to be found in the Atharva-Veda-Jyotish, the probable date of which, according to Dixit and others, is 900 to 1500 BC.'

From the mass of evidence, of which the above is only representative, it seems reasonable to infer that India was indebted to neither the Greeks nor the Moslems for its astrological doctrines, but rather to its own sages who lived in prehistoric times, for its learning and proficiency. It is not impossible—in fact, there is considerable supporting evidence in the literary fragments of the classical pagans—that the entire structure of Chaldean, Egyptian, Greek and Roman learning, especially the more occult sciences,

was originally derived from Asia. It is recorded of both the Egyptian Osiris and the Greek Orpheus that they were 'dark skinned men' from the East, who brought the first knowledge of the sacred sciences from a race or order of sages who passed an almost fabled existence amidst the highlands of northern Hindustan. The Chinese have a similar record as to the source of their metaphysical culture, for reference is made in the sacred literature of the Tian-Ta'i sect to 'The Great Teachers of the Snowy Mountains, the school of the Haimavatas,' and also to 'The great professors of the highest order who live in mountain depths remote from men.'

There is an old Hindu legend which brings out a very subtle phase of astrological philosophy. Vishnu, the second person of the Hindu triad, while reposing calmly on his heavenly throne, thought of casting a look at his own nativity, and found in it that the next 19 years of his life were under the malefic influence of Saturn.

So, in order if possible to evade it, and to defeat Saturn, Vishnu transformed himself into the shape of an elephant and spent the 19 years in a dense forest, eating grass and other vegetables, fearing lest Saturn would inflict on him insufferable punishment had he remained in his divine shape.

When the 19 years had elapsed, Vishnu resumed his real form and throne, and while sitting there he one day saw Saturn passing by, and calling to him, asked: 'How was it, Saturn, that you were not able to do me any injury in the 19 years in which you had power over me?'

'Why sir,' replied Saturn, 'what can we poor subordinates do to such exalted gods as you are, except that for 19 years you have been eating nothing but grass, and passing a most miserable life indeed, tormented by flies and mosquitoes.'

The horoscope of Rama is an exceedingly fitting example of Hindu astrology and is preserved by Valmiki in the eighteenth chapter of the *Bala Kanda*. The data is given as follows: 'Rama was born in Kataka with Chundra and Buru there, Sani in Thula, Kuja in Makara, Sukra in Meena, Ravi in Mesha and Buda in Vrishabha.' Translated into English, this means that Cancer was rising, with the Moon in conjunction with Jupiter in the same sign. Saturn was in Libra, Mars in Capricorn, Venus in Pisces, the Sun in Aries and Mercury in Taurus. The Dragon Head is calculated in Sagittarius. According to Sepharial, it is probable that the horoscope is of a man born prior to 3102 BC, and under such conditions would be one of the earliest horoscopes available for public examination.

It should be noted that Hindu astrology differs from that of Ptolemy in one very definite particular. The Oriental calculations are based upon what has been termed a natural zodiac, while that of Western people is based upon what is called an intellectual zodiac. Approximately 1400 years have passed since these two zodiacs coincided, and there is now a discrepancy of some 20 degrees between the two systems. The Oriental zodiac is, therefore, about 20 degrees behind the Ptolemaic, and in applying Hindu keywords to horoscopes set up according to the Western methods, this difference must be taken into consideration.

GREECE AND ROME

According to EA Wallis-Budge, Nectanebus was the last of the native kings of ancient Egypt. He was learned in all the transcendental arts and devoted to astrology. His occult knowledge enabled Nectanebus to circumvent the numerous conspirators who plotted his destruction.

He left Egypt because the gods of that country would no longer render their assistance to his magical operations, and took up residence among the Macedonians in the guise of the god Ammon. He in turn spun the web of sorcery about Alexander the Great, whose claims to a 'divine' origin are probably founded upon this circumstance.

When the time came for Olympias to give birth to her son, Nectanebus was present in the role of an astrologer. Standing beside the queen, he calculated the positions of the heavenly bodies and besought her not to permit the child to be born until the most auspicious moment had arrived. 'It was not until he saw a certain splendor in the sky and knew that all the heavenly bodies were in a favorable position that he permitted her to bring forth her child.'

At the birth of Alexander at 9:26 pm (local time) on 1 July 357 BC, is is reported that the earth was shaken, the heavens were

ALEXANDER M.

Above: **Alexander the Great. Born on 1 July 357 AD, at 9:26 pm, this great conqueror was a Cancer. Nectanebus—a sorcerer who had gained the ear of Queen Olympia, Alexander's mother—convinced the queen to delay the moment of Alexander's birth until the most propitious hour, according to the stars.** *At right:* **The temple of Apollo at Delphi. Apollo was, to the ancient Greek mind, the God of the Sun. Greek astrology was influenced by the Platonic doctrine that the heavenly bodies were beings.**

filled with fires and thunders crashed through the deep. At the instant the babe was delivered, Nectanebus exclaimed: 'O Queen, now thou wilt give birth to a governor of the world!'

The nobility of Plato's intellect; the estimation in which his writings are held by all civilized peoples; and the significant fact that we are indebted to him for the first allusion to astrology in Greek literature, all amply justify the publication of his horoscope as a most noble fragment of this ancient learning.

In his *De Nativitatibus* of seven centuries later, Julius Firmicus Maternus calculated the horoscope of this remarkable man. The scheme of the nativity is given as follows: 'If the Ascendant shall be Aquarius, Mars, Mercury and Venus therein posited; and if Jupiter then be placed in the seventh, having Leo for his sign, and in the second the Sun in Pisces and the Moon in fifth House, beholding the Ascendant with a trine aspect, and Saturn in the ninth from the Ascendant in Libra. This Geniture renders a Man Interpreter of Divine and heavenly Institutions, who endued with instructive speech, and the power of Divine Wit, and formed in a manner by a celestial Institution, by the true License of disputations shall arrive at all the secrets of Divinity.'

The horoscope as set up by Firmicus is extremely probable. The sign in which the Sun is placed agrees with Plato's physical appearance, as does the ascendant with the qualities of mind. Pisces confers heaviness and breadth, and 'Aristo named him *Plato* (which implieth Latitude) in allusion to the largeness of his person; others say, to the wideness of his shoulders.' Neanthes relates the term to the breadth of his forehead.

Jupiter, the ruler of Pisces, when powerful, gives the 'divine appearance,' and, according to Hesychius, the philosopher was

called *Serapis* from the majesty and dignity of his person. Aquarius was termed the sign of the truth-seeker, and of all men it may be said of Plato that he lived for truth alone. The serenity of Plato's mind, the earnestness of his endeavor, the synthesis which marks his classification of facts, the humaneness and rationality of his soul—all these qualities, perfected by the magnificent inclusiveness of his erudition, reveal the highly developed Aquarian type.

In his commentary on this Platonic doctrine, Proclus observes that the length of the great year is determined by conjunctions of the planets. He notes that the sign of Cancer is the ascendant of the world horoscope and that a period of the universe is that time which must elapse between conjunctions of all the planets in this sign. The vast interval of time between such conjunctions is divisible into a number of lesser periods, each of which, resulting from a different harmony of the heavenly bodies, is distinguished from the others by the modifications which it causes in the productiveness of nature.

Referring to Plato's universal cycle, Thorndike, in his *History of Magic and Experimental Science*, notes that 'history begins to repeat itself in every detail when the heavenly bodies have regained their original positions.' Aristotle concurs with his master in recognizing the heavenly bodies as superhuman, intelligent, incorporate deities. The difference between this viewpoint and astrology is almost imperceptible, for, according to Diodorus, the Chaldeans taught that 'every event in the heavens has its meaning, as part of the eternal scheme of divine forethought.' Theophrastus, who succeeded Aristotle in the peripatetic school, was even more

outspoken in his admiration for astrology. Proclus reports him as saying, 'The most extraordinary thing of his age was the lore of the Chaldeans, who foretold not only events of public interest but even the lives and deaths of individuals.'

Seneca is in accord with the Chaldean Berosus, who declared that 'whenever all the stars are in conjunction in the sign of Cancer, there will be a universal conflagration, and a second deluge when they all unite in Capricorn.'

The astral philosophy of the Greeks was most certainly derived from that of the Far East. We cannot do better than to accept Stanley's summary of the origins of Greek learning: 'Although some Grecians have challenged to their nation the original of philosophy, yet the more learned of them have acknowledged it derived from the East. To omit the dark traditions of the Athenians concerning Musaeus, of the Thebanes, concerning Linus, and of the Thracians about Orpheus, it is manifest that the original of the Greek philosophy is to be derived from Thales, who, traveling into the East, first brought Natural learning, Geometry and Astrology thence into Greece, for which reason the attribute of Wise was conferred upon him, and at the same time upon six others for their eminence in morality and politics.'

The story of the influence of astrology upon the Roman Empire is a history of Rome itself. The emperor Numa was addicted to all forms of magical arts. HP Blavatsky, in his *The Secret Doctrine*, relates that, 'Marcus Antonius never traveled without an astrologer recommended to him by Cleopatra.'

Before his ascent to the throne, Augustus Caesar went to the astrologer Theogenes, who fell on his knees before the youth and predicted his rise to power. Augustus was so impressed that he published his horoscope and had a silver coin struck with the sign of Capricorn, under which he was born, upon one of its surfaces.

The astrologers Thracyllus, the Elder and Thracyllus, the Younger were constantly consulted by both the emperors Tiberius and Nero. 'Tiberius, who believed in nothing else except thunderstorms, placed unbounded faith in the Chaldeans (astrologers),' notes Granger in *Worship of the Romans*.

He had studied the art under Thracyllus, whom he put to a severe test. Tiberius himself also reached a high pitch of proficiency. He foretold that Galba would one day reign, and in his last hours revealed the career of his successor, Gaius. According to Seneca, 'A meteor "as big as the Moon appeared when Paulus was engaged in the war against Perseus"; similar portents marked the death of Augustus and execution of Sejanus, and gave warning of the death of Germanicus.'

Sylla, the astrologer and mathematician, read the horoscope of Caligula, revealing to Caesar the time and conditions under which he would die. This same emperor was admonished by the Sortes Antiatinae that 'he should beware of Cassius,' and by the conspiracy and sword of a man of this name he died. Otho surrounded himself with seers and astrologers, and sought advice from Ptolemy, being assured by the latter that he should outlive Nero and be a ruler of the Romans.

Nero himself practiced astrology. Vitellius was left upon the horns of a dilemma: He attempted to banish the astrologers from Rome—that is, all except his own—but these 'Chaldeans' outwitted him, for they published a proclamation to the effect that the day of their banishment would also be that upon which the emperor died. Vitellius was so terrified by the prognostication that he permitted them to remain undisturbed.

Selenus gave warnings to Vespasian (who consulted his stars daily). Apollonius, the astrologer-magician of Tyana, was also admired and his advice sought by Vespasian, Titus and Nerva, but viewed with dismay by Nero and Domitian, who were terrified by his wisdom and power. Domitian would make no important move of any kind without consulting his stars.

Adrian, who was adept in astrology, wrote from the stars a diary of his own life, even predicting the hour of his own death, all this long before the incidents themselves actually occurred. Septimus Severus caused his horoscope to be inscribed upon the roof of his judicial palace with the statement of his foreknowledge that he would not return alive from his expedition to England. He died at York, in accordance with his own prophetic knowledge.

We have already noted that Constantine the Great believed in his stars, and the astrologer Heliodorus was the adviser of the emperor Valens. Julian, one of the most scholarly of the Roman emperors, wrote that in his youth he had been a student of astrology. The historian Ammianus Marcellinus also testified to Julian's devotion to the occult sciences.

A curious early manuscript entitled *Tabulae Frisicae* contains the horoscope of Romulus attributed to Ptolemy. The rarity of this nativity justifies its publication as an important fragment of Roman astrology.

Varro, the distinguished Roman scholar, requested his friend, Lucius Tarutius Firmanus, one of the most renowned of Roman astrologers, to cast the horoscope of the Eternal City. Firmanus reported that the walls of Rome were begun by Romulus in the twenty-second year of his age, on the eleventh day of May, between the second and third hours. At that time, the Sun was in Taurus, the Moon in Libra, Saturn in Scorpio, Jupiter in Pisces, Mars in Scorpio, Venus in Scorpio and Mercury in Scorpio. Firmanus, who placed great reliance in the lunar motion, used this data to predict the destiny of Rome.

At top, above: The ancient Greek Pantheon, clockwise from the top: Ares, Eros, Aphrodite, Zeus, Pallas Athena, Apollo, Demeter, Poseidon, Hephaestos, Selena, Hermes, Hera, and Artemis.

The Romans took much of the Greek Pantheon for their own, and named the gods in their Roman equivalent of the Greek. Therefore, we have *above*, a Roman zodiac with Mercury (Hermes), Minerva (Athena), Cupid (Eros) and Jupiter (Zeus). *At right:* The Portico of Octavian at the Roman Forum.

To appreciate the veneration accorded by Romans to those proficient in astrological lore, we cannot do better than to summarize in the words of Vitruvius: 'Their learning deserves the admiration of mankind.'

The eclectic spirit prevailing in Rome caused the Eternal City to become a center for the exchange of ideas—religious, philosophic and political. The temples of various gods were clustered together in the Forum. In this cosmopolitan atmosphere astrology gained

many converts among the powerful, the wealthy and the wise. Several new titles were bestowed upon the stargazers. They were called *astrologi*, *mathematici* and *genethliaci*.

The origin of the science caused those proficient in it to also be termed *Chaldaei*, or *Babylonii*. In writings of this period, therefore, astrologers of all nationalities were known as *Chaldeans*, and are so described by Hippolytus, who makes grudging reference to their abilities. According to HP Blavatsky in *The Secret Doctrine*, 'Under the wisest emperors, Rome had a School of Astrology, wherein were secretly taught the occult influences of Sun, Moon and Saturn.' Even when the astrologers fell upon evil times, they continued to flourish.

Though Hadrian applied himself to astrology and magical arts in order to enjoy the extensions of knowledge they bestowed, he sought at the same time to prevent others from improving their fortunes by applying themselves to such sciences. It is now generally conceded that it was by the aid of the prophetic waters of the Kastalian spring that Hadrian came to the imperial chair. 'We may recall,' writes WR Halliday in *Greek Divination*, 'the attitude of the Roman emperors toward astrology. If the stars merely reveal the future, what harm could the astrologer effect? Yet to prophesy the emperor's death was a capital offense. (Queen Elizabeth I caused similar legislation to be enacted in England.) Hadrian is said to have blocked up the Kastalian spring because he had learned his imperial destiny from its prophetic water and feared that others might consult it for a similar purpose.'

In their extremely superficial examination of astrological phenomena, modern psychologists have attempted to explain away the science by maintaining that predictions bring about their own fulfillment. But here again is a dilemma. Take, for example, the story of the Greek tragic poet Aeschylus who, discovering from his stars that he would die at a certain time by an object falling upon him, sought to escape his destiny by remaining in the desert until after the fatal aspect had passed. Seating himself in an open place, with nothing but the blue sky above him Aeshylus felt himself reasonably secure. But a great bird, mistaking the poet's bald head for a rock, dropped a turtle upon it to break its shell, thereby killing Aeschylus and fulfilling the prediction.

Other similar cases are recorded in which the stars have vindicated themselves in extraordinary ways. Michael Scott, the astrologer and confidant of Emperor Frederick II, predicted that he himself would die from a rock hitting him on the head. Scott was killed by a loose stone that fell from the roof of the cathedral while he knelt in prayer. Franciscus Junctinus, a Florentine astrologer, also predicted for himself a violent death, and upon the very hour foretold was killed when some heavy books fell upon him as he sat in his library.

No more dramatic incident is recorded in the history of Rome than the interview between Agrippina, the mother of Nero, and the Chaldean astrologer. This scheming woman sought the advice of the stars as to the outcome of her life's ambition to make her son the emperor of the Romans. The astrologer cast the nativity and rendered the following judgment: 'If he reigns, he shall kill his mother.'

Without a moment's hesitation, Agrippina, with teeth set, hissed back the answer: 'Let him kill me so that he but reigns!'

Needless to say, the stars gave honest judgment.

In later years, Nero surrounded himself with astrologers, and Bamilus was not only his constant adviser but repeatedly warned the emperor that his reckless course was bringing him to an untimely end.

No consideration of astrology during the Roman period should omit reference to the opinions of the Alexandrian Platonists—Plotinus and Proclus are pre-eminent. Porphyry and Iamblichus

At top, above: **The temple of Jupiter at Olympia.** *Above:* **A view of the Roman Forum.** *At right:* **A Roman cosmos—with scenes from their mythology encircling the signs of the zodiac—decorates this dish, which dates from 360 AD. Dormant during the Middle Ages, astrology made a comeback.**

also merit mention. According to Plotinus, as quoted in Thorndike's *History of Magic and Experimental Science*: 'It is abundantly evident… that the motion of the heavens affects things on Earth.'

Golden-souled Proclus, designated as the Platonic Successor, who succeeded Syrianus in the rectorship of the Platonic School at Athens, wrote a paraphrase of Ptolemy's *Tetrabiblos*, which was so excellent that Melanchthon found it worthy of publication, although only the previous year he had republished Camerarius' edition of the same work with original emendations. Proclus also prepared several commentaries upon the astronomical and astrological precepts of Ptolemy, which amply set forth his attitude about such matters.

Porphyry also relates that when he had resolved to kill himself, Plotinus read his intentions in the stars and dissuaded him from following through.

THE ARABIANS

The Arabians possessed an avid yearning to acquire knowledge, and they actively studied other great cultures to glean what they could from them. However, with the fall of Rome, Western Europe—a major seat of learning—was in a state of seige, with Germanic tribes from the north, and Slavs from the east, rapidly dismantling what had been the Western Roman empire.

The Christian Church sought to preserve civilization, but its unified model for Europe was long overcome by the tribal ideal of the barbarians, just as the Roman trial by reason and evidence was at odds with the barbarian trial by ordeal. Even with Christianity,

Germanic peoples preferred fiefdoms—thus, Europe became a synthesis of Germanic feudal states unified solely by Christian theology. Monasteries became seats of learning, especially in the British Isles. The monks fought superstition, taught the locals better farming and building methods and encouraged Christian spiritual life and learning.

However, with the fragmentary nature of feudalism, Europe was rocked by repeated invasions and feuding, only to rise time and again—with the illustrious ninth-century court of Charlemagne, and, in the twelfth and thirteenth centuries, with the rise of villages (the 'grid system' is a medieval invention) and states.

The Eastern Roman Empire was established as a Christian empire by the Roman emperor Constantine (himself a non-Christian until his baptism in old age), after a dream in which he was told he would conquer under the sign of the cross. This empire lasted for 1000 years, roughly the extent of the medieval period.

The Eastern Empire, known as 'Byzantium,' was a synthesis of Christian theology and Greek social order, and preserved, without obstacle, classical learning. St Basil, himself a renowned philosopher who converted to monastic Christianity, evidenced this in his book *To The Young: How They Might Derive Profit From the Reading of Pagan Literature*, in which he expounds on reading Greek and Roman classics with a discerning Christian eye.

The Empire's capitol city, Constantinople, was situated at the mouth of the Strait of Bosphorus, between the Mediterranean and the Black Sea. Renowned for its architectural, spiritual and intellectual glory, all nations brought their trade to Constantinople—also from whence went envoys to all regions of the Eastern Empire's extensive dominion.

The Arabians came to the Eastern Empire for knowledge, even with a jihad, or holy war, against all peoples that were not Moslems. Hence, the Aristotelian logic behind the Persian-Arabian astronomer Avicenna's renowned *Proof of the Existence of God*.

Astrology had its resurgence in Europe via the Arabian Moors. With the Moorish conquest of Spain during the most fragmented period of the European Middle Ages, some European scholars turned to them for knowledge. The celebrated Caliph Al-Raschid was given to astrology, and *The Thousand and one Arabian Nights* tales abound with references to astrology and astromancy. Al-Rashid ordered the astronomical books of Ptolemy translated into Arabic.

In his *Manual of Astrology*, the nineteenth century English astrologer Raphael (RC Smith) gives several examples of predictions made and advice given to the emperors of this house. Raphael sums up his historical review of astrology and magic in Islam as follows: 'These sciences were circulated amongst the different Arabian tribes, by whom they were much respected as in Egypt. Indeed, the respect entertained for them by the Arabians in general contributed in a great degree to the success of Mohammed. In his life we see the favorable predictions of many very celebrated astrologers of his time; and among others, that of *Eukeaz*, who told the uncle of the 'Prophet' that all circumstances in his infancy conspired to announce that he would be a very extraordinary man, and that his life should be guarded with the most vigilant attention. As also the prediction of another, no less famous in the art, who on being presented to him at Bassora, took Mohammed by the hand and exclaimed with transport, "Behold the Lord of the World, the Mercy of the Universe." '

The astrology of the Arabs was derived from numerous and widely separated sources. It is generally accepted that its Grecian background was derived principally from Ptolemy, Bettius Valens, Dorotheus Sidonius, Teucer and Antiochus. A considerable part was also drawn from Persian and Indian books and from the oral traditions of Mesopotamia, Syria and Egypt.

In their astrological philosophy, the Muslim peoples are essentially eclectic, but in one particular they departed from the older systems. They perfected the mathematical aspect of astrology, achieving a high degree of accuracy in spherical trigonometry and other advanced mathematical sciences. The Arabs also devised numerous tables for the calculation of nativities and reduced a vast astrological lore to an orderly and systematic procedure. They formulated many of the terms now used in astrological literature, creating a considerable vocabulary to distinguish the nomenclature of this science from that of other forms of learning.

The Arabian astrologers became proficient not only in natal astrology but in predictions relating to cities, races, religions and other mundane, horary and electional subjects as well. Predictions were successfully made from eclipses of the Sun and Moon, comets and other celestial phenomena.

Their technical name for astrology is 'The Science of the

Above: **The Persian astronomer Avicenna (980–1037) avidly sought knowledge from the great eastern Christian capitol of Constantinople.**

Decrees of the Stars.' The astrologer is called Ah-Kami, or Munadjdjim, the latter name *also* signifying an astronomer. Indeed, it was not until the nineteenth century that any precise distinction was made between an astronomer and an astrologer—and each was presumed to possess the knowledge peculiar to the other.

The Arabs recognized the importance of astrology in physiology and medicine. In this they accepted the opinions of Hippocrates and developed a considerable science of planetary cycles, climatic periods and critical days. The opinions of the Arabs in these matters are preserved for European astrologers in Culpeper's *Semeiotica Uranica*. This noted astrologer, physician and herbalist derives much of the contents of this work from the treatise of the Arabian physician Ibraham Avenezra in *Critical Days*.

ANCIENT MIDDLE AMERICA

There is abundant evidence in the hieroglyphical figures of the ancient people of Central America—and the commentaries about them by the early Spanish priests—that they had developed elaborate systems of natal and judicial astrology.

Prescott, in his *History of the Conquest of Mexico*, notes that the Aztecs, when a child was born into their nation, instantly summoned an adivino (astrologer) whose duty it was to ascertain the destiny of the newborn babe. 'The sign,' wrote Lucien Biart, 'that marked the day of his birth was noted, and also the one that ruled during the period of the last 13 years. If the child was born at midnight, they compared the preceding day and the day following.'

Like the Greeks, Egyptians and other ancient peoples, the augurs among the Mexicans foretold events from the positions of the planets, the arrangements of sacred numbers, from clouds, storms, eclipses, comets, the flight of birds and the actions of animals. Their astrological knowledge was derived principally from the doctrines and revelations of Quetzalcoatl, the first and foremost of their philosophers and teachers.

Quetzalcoatl was the Son of Heaven. His true parent was the Universal Creator in the dual aspect of father-mother. In the physi-

Above: An Aztec calendar stone (see also page 31). The Aztec calendar
displays the Aztec cosmos, and shares its origin with the Mayan calendar, and features a familiar blend of cosmological and mythological symbols.

cal world he was born of the Virgin Sochiquetzal, and his coming was annunciated by a heavenly apparition, which declared that it had come as an ambassador from the god of the Milky Way to discover among mortals the blessed Virgin who was to become the mother of the Divine Incarnation.

Among the appellations of the god Quetzalcoatl, therefore, are 'He who was born of the Virgin,' 'Lord of the Winds' and 'priest-prophet-king.' The astrology of the Aztecs was thus derived from the highest authority, and from Quetzalcoatl the knowledge of the starry science descended through a sacerdotal line of initiated priest-philosophers. Quetzalcoatl himself devised the astrological cycle and the *Tonalamatl*—the *Book of the Fates of Man*.

The Spanish writer Mendietam gives a brief description of the manner in which Quetzalcoatl came to originate the sacred astrological calendar. He says that 'the gods thought it well that the people should have some means of writing by which they might

direct themselves, and two of their number, Oxomoco and Cipactonal, who dwelt in a cave in Cuernavaca, especially considered the matter.

'Cipactonal thought that her descendent Quetzalcoatl should be consulted and she called him into counsel. He, too, thought the idea of the calendar good, and the three addressed themselves to the task of making the *Tonalamatl*, or Book of Fate. to Cipactonal was given the privilege of choosing and writing the first sign, or day-symbol, of the calendar. She painted the *Cipactli*, or dragon animal, and called the sign *Ce Cipactli* ("one *Cipactli*"). Oxomoco then wrote *Om Acatl* ("two canes") and Quetzalcoatl "three houses" and so on, until the thirteen signs were completed.'

In ancient Mexico, as in other parts of the civilized world, astrology was cultivated not by the ignorant and superstitious but by the great and learned. Three of the great names in the whole history of the Aztec nation are intimately connected with this science—Quetzalcoatl, Nazahualpilli and Montezuma. Nazahualpilli was the king of Tezcuco. Of this king, Torquemada writes in the second book of *The Indian Monarchy*, 'They say that he was a great astrologer and prided himself much on his knowledge of the motions of the celestial bodies; and being attached to this study, that he caused inquiries to be made throughout the entire of his dominions, for all such persons as were at all conversant with it, whom he brought to his court, and imparted to them whatever he knew; and ascending by night on the terraced roof of his palace, he thence considered the stars, and disputed with them on all difficult questions concerned with them.

'I at least can affirm that I have seen a place on the outside of the roof of the palace, enclosed within four walls only a yard in height, and just of sufficient breadth for a man to lie down in; in each angle of which was a hole or perforation, in which was placed a lance, upon which was hung a sphere; and upon inquiring the use of this square space, a grandson of his, who was showing me the palace, replied that it was for King Nazahualpilli when he went by night, attended by his astrologers, to contemplate the heavens and the stars.'

Lord Kinsborough, the author of *Antiquities of Mexico*, one of the greatest of all works on Mexican antiquities, says that it can hardly be doubted that these Indians were acquainted with many scientific instruments. The thirteenth plate of Dupaix's *The Monuments of New Spain* reproduces an ancient figure representing a man holding something resembling a telescope to one of his eyes. It was King Nazahualpilli who stood before Montezuma when that young man ascended to the throne of Mexico and congratulated the whole nation on the election of a king 'whose deep knowledge of heavenly things insured to his subjects his comprehension of those of an earthly nature.'

Montezuma was the most outstanding organizing genius of the Aztec world. He conquered 44 cities, binding them to his rule so that they paid tribute to him and acknowledged vassalage. This last king of the Indians was not only a great general, statesman and prince, but also a distinguished patron of the occult arts, especially astrology.

In his *Mexico, A Study of Two Americas*, Stuart Chase relates that, 'In astronomy the American mind reached its climax, and the Mayas were its high priests. Starting with observations of the heavens some 4000 years ago, the Mayan calendar was developed

Below: **An Aztec pyramid, from the top of which one might view the stars.** *At right:* **An illustration and explanation of the Aztec calendar.**

The 20 signs of the Aztec zodiac:

1.	Cipactli	The Crocodile	7.	Macatl	The Deer
2.	Eecatl	The Wind	8.	Tochtli	The Rabbit
3.	Calli	The House	9.	Atl	The Water
4.	Cuelzpalin	The Lizard	10.	Itzcuintli	The Dog
5.	Couatl	The Snake	11.	Ocomatli	The Monkey
6.	Miquizli	Death	12.	Malinalli	The Twisted
			13.	Actl	The Reed
			14.	Ocelotl	The Jaguar

15.	Quauhtli	The Vulture
16.	Cozcaquauhili	The Eagle
17.	Olin	Motion (the Sun)
18.	Tecpatl	The Flint Knife
19.	Quiauitl	The Rain
20.	Xochitl	The Flower

In the center of the calendar are the Sun, Moon and five stars. Among the Aztec deities are six which they call 'wanderers,' and we may infer that these gods were connected with the planets. As Jupiter is the sacred planet for the time cycles of the Tibetans, so Venus, the start of Quetzalcoatl, is the sacred planet of the time cycles of the Mexicans. The Mayans also observed the time cycle of Mars.

to a point where it was possible to distinguish, without duplication, any given day in 370,000 years! This was far in advance of European astronomy, more accurate than anything so-called Western civilization achieved until very recent times. The Aztecs borrowed Mayan principles but never achieved such mathematical elegance. Their solar calendar, however, was more accurate than that of the Spaniards. They were found in full knowledge of the year of Venus, eclipses, solstices, equinoxes and such phenomena.... It is not unreasonable to suppose that, during these 150 years, (450 to 600 AD) the Mayas were the most civilized people on the planet.'

The astrological systems of the Aztecs and the other nations of Central America and Yucatan are evidently identical in origin with that of the Mayans, differing only in minor details from those of the more northern Indians. Alexander von Humboldt, an authority on these subjects, has pointed out the numerous correspondences which exist between the astrological symbols of the Mexicans and those of the Chaldeans, Greeks and Egyptians. Though present knowledge of Aztec metaphysics is extremely fragmentary, one may dimly perceive something of the vastness and profundity of their theories. It may yet be demonstrated that their knowledge of the occult forces working in nature was scarcely less complete than that of the Eastern Hemisphere.

The Indians assigned special virtues to the hours, days, weeks, months, years and other great cycles of 52 years, which they termed 'bundles.' The day cycle consisted of 13 hours, the fifth hour being noon, so that the number seven was regarded with special veneration. The gods ruling over the diurnal period are

Below and at right: Late afternoon views of an ancient Central American observatory—the Great Caracole at Chichen Itza. King Nazahualpilli, ruler of the Aztec city of Tezcuco, a strong adherent of Aztec astrology, went to the roof of his palace every night, to observe the stars in the company of his astrologers.

The Aztecs believed in good days and bad days, good hours and bad hours and had two annual calendars—a judicial year and a sacred year. The judicial year was composed of 18 months of 20 days each for a total of 365 days, 52 of which constituted an entire cycle. The sacred year was composed of 20 months of 13 days each for a total of 260 days.

As with the Egyptians and Hindus, deities and virtues were assigned to various months in the Aztec sacred calendar, with that influence going through various permutations throughout the 13-day month. That may explain some of the rather esoteric practices that the Aztecs performed in sacrificial rites. Perhaps it depended on the 'deity of the month.'

Interestingly, there is at least one ancient Aztec motif that depicts a man holding a telescope-like instrument to his eye. Certainly, the Aztecs spent a good deal of time stargazing, and Montezuma, the last of the Aztec emperors, studied astrology assiduously, even up to the time the *Conquistadors* brought down his nation and roasted the emperor himself on a spit.

It has been said that the Aztecs perfected the art of Central American astrology, and that their concept of monthly influences was similar to the complex concepts of the Egyptians.

elaborately pictured in the Aztec books and are termed collectively the Lords of the Day. The Aztec night consisted of nine periods, the fifth period being midnight, so that the numeral five was accepted as an evil symbol. The Spaniards referred to the nine nocturnal divinities as 'Senores de las Noches'—Lords of the Night.

The various hours of both day and night were demonstrated as good, bad and indifferent, and each hour had a god which ruled over it. To the Aztec astrologers, to be born in the first hour of the night was fortunate, the second hour unfortunate, the third hour fortunate again, the fourth hour indifferent, and so forth. These Lords of the Day and Night correspond with the planetary hour deities of the Chaldeans.

The *Tonalamatl* set forth a perpetual calendar of beneficial and malefic periods. This work was not only consulted at the birth of a child, but was also used as a textbook of electional astrology, from which was determined auspicious periods for the commencement of enterprises for the accomplishment of any desired end. The *Tonalamatl* combines in one volume cosmogony and divination, a circumstance which has induced modern writers on the subject of the Aztec civilization to admit that an understanding of this book is essential to a full appreciation of the arts, philosophies and sciences of these Indians.

The Aztecs had both a judicial and sacred year. The judicial year consisted of 365 days and was arranged in 18 months of 20 days each, with five inter-calendary days that were nameless and unfortunate. No man performed labor which could be avoided upon these five days; to be born upon one of them was a disaster; and men began no enterprise upon them lest it fail. Fifty-two of these 365-day years constituted a cycle, and it is now believed that although the Mayans carried their time calculations into vast cycles of time, the Aztecs had no method of chronology beyond the 52-year cycle.

The sacred year—the one set forth in the *Tonalamatl* of Quetzalcoatl—consisted of but 260 days. These were divided into 20 periods of 13 days each. These 20 periods were termed months. Seventy-three of these sacred years of 260 days each were equal to 52 years of the 365-day years, and thus the two calendars were reconciled.

The zodiac began at the upper right side of a wheel, with the first sign being the Crocodile. It then proceeds clockwise in the order of the dots, reaching 13, where it begins with 1 again and continues to 7. The dots here form a key to the cycles, for if a given month begins with the Crocodile and continues for 13 days, it will end in the sign of the Jaguar, and will then continue in a clockwise direction for 13, ending in the sign of the Skeleton (Death). The next month will begin with the Deer, the sign directly following the Skeleton, and continue clockwise in this manner until 20 such cycles of 13 days have been completed, when it will be evident that the count will return to the starting point—the Crocodile. This constitutes the Tonalamatl cycle.

Each of the months of 13 days is under the general control of the deity and virtue which rules its first day, or beginning, and the other 12 days of that month are modifications of this first influence. This procedure is somewhat similar to the decan theory and minor divisions of astrological signs used by the Egyptians and Hindus.

At left: **The Great Caracole at Chichen Itza. It is oriented facing the setting point of the planet Venus, which was the celestial manifestation of the Toltec deity Quetzalcoatl. The second story was aligned with the Venusian positions as morning and evening star. The third story was given over to window alignments coinciding with horizon events, including various settings of Venus, sunset and sunrise on the equinoxes.**

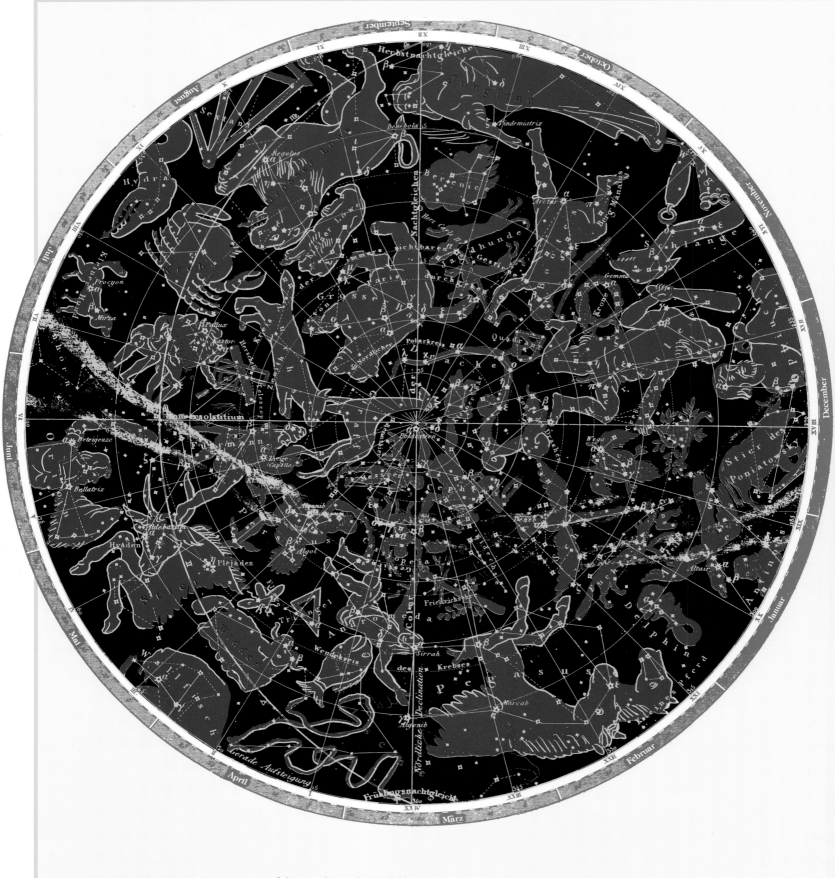

Above: **A nineteenth-century German map of the northern sky, with the signs of the Zodiac—among the other constellations. Counterclockwise from the top, the signs of the Zodiac are: Jungfrau (Virgo, the virgin); the Grosser Lowe (Leo, the lion); Krebs (Cancer, the crab); Zwillinge (Gemini, the twins); Stier (Taurus, the bull); and Widder (Aries, the ram).**

Above: This is the southern sky counterpart to the map on the opposite page. Counterclockwise from the top, we once again begin with Jungfrau, or Virgo, and then proceed on through the zodiacal signs that are unique to this map—Waage (Libra, the scales); Skorpion (Scorpio, the scorpion); Schutze (Sagittarius, the archer); Steinbock (Capricorn, the sea-goat); Wassermann (Aquarius, the water carrier); and Fische (Pisces, the fish).

THE ESSENCE OF ASTROLOGY

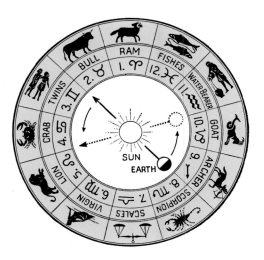

Astrology can be defined as that ancient science which describes the influence of the stars upon Nature and mankind. A horoscope is a map or diagram of the heavens cast for a particular moment of time and read according to well-established rules. The horoscope is calculated by a mathematical process—free from the elements of chance or divination. Predictions are deduced from the horoscope in a strict mathematical way. To quote Rapahel's *A Manual of Astrology*, 'according to a certain chain of causes which for ages past have been found uniformly to produce a correspondent train of effects.'

As practiced by various authorities in various countries, there are two fundamentally different methods, or approaches, to astrology: the geocentric and the heliocentric. Geocentric astrology is based upon calculations of the planetary positions as seen by the observer on the Earth, ie, using the Earth as a center. Heliocentric astrology bases its interpretations upon positions within the solar system with reference to the Sun as the center. While it is true that the Sun is the center, the effect of the motion—as manifest on Earth—is the basis of most astrological interpretation. Therefore, the vast majority of astrologers employ the geocentric calculations of the planets' positions.

However, these terms are used by many astrologers in a different sense, ie, heliocentric when considering changes of position

At left: **A deep space closeup of Sagittarius, showing the Lagoon Nebula.**

by virtue of the body's motion in orbit, and geocentric when considering changes in position with reference to the observer, by reason of the observer's orbit around the Earth—the revolution of the periphery of the Earth around the Earth's center. The astrological signs are heliocentric divisions, or heliarcs, while the houses of the zodiac are geocentric divisions, or geoarcs.

The zodiac was said in ancient times to extend some eight degrees on each side of the ecliptic. Modern astronomers have widened it to nine degrees on either side because of the extreme latitudes which Venus and Mars attain. The position of any planet within, or of any star within or outside of the zodiac, is measured by a perpendicular to the ecliptic. The point where their perpendicular meets the ecliptic is the geocentric longitude of the star or planet. In a sense, the zodiac is identical with the ecliptic, for both are measured from a point of beginning at the Vernal Equinox.

The annual revolution of the Earth around the Sun is divided into 360 degrees of a circle, a division that mathematically and astronomically is universally accepted. The subdivisions of the circle into 12 equal arcs, distinguished by names, are known as the signs of the zodiac. They no longer bear any but the most rudimentary relationship to the constellations of the same names.

These arcs are measured from the point where the Sun crosses the celestial equator at the beginning of Spring, on or about 21 March each year. As this is coincidental with the position of the Earth's axis at right angles to the radius of its orbit, the days and nights are of equal duration all over the Earth. The point is termed the Vernal Equinox. That the zodiacal year seems at one period of history to have begun with Taurus indicates that these records date from between 2000 and 4000 BC, during which period the equinoctial point fell in Taurus.

The further fact that the Equinox still continues to fall in zero degrees in Aries, indicates that at some time since the beginning of the Christian era the fixed zodiac of constellations was abandoned and the names reapplied to a moving zodiac, based upon the equinoctial point then recognized as the beginning of the astrological year. The year's arc of precession was thus ignored—an annual loss of a moment of time that shows up in no calculation presently in use, other than in a consideration of the precession of the equinoctial point and the one degree revision of star positions every 70 years.

Thus, for at least 40 centuries, astrologers have recognized the receding point of the node of intersection of the ecliptic and the celestial equator as the commencement of a scheme of magnetic conditioning.

Persons born 'on the line' between two signs of the zodiac partake of qualities found in both those signs, or more strictly speaking, have a blend of traits that may compose an individual nature. Due to variations in astrological calendars, this may become apparent during the last few days of a departing sign, but the 'cusp,' as it is termed, pertains chiefly to the first week of the incoming sign. While the new sign is gaining its ascendancy, the

The four basic groups:

Fire Signs: The Inspirational Group
Water Signs: The Emotional Group
Air Signs: The Mental Group
Earth Signs: The Practical Group

The elements of the four basic groups:

	Cardinal	Fixed	Mutable
Fire:	Aries	Leo	Sagittarius
Water:	Cancer	Scorpio	Pisces
Air:	Libra	Aquarius	Gemini
Earth:	Capricorn	Taurus	Virgo

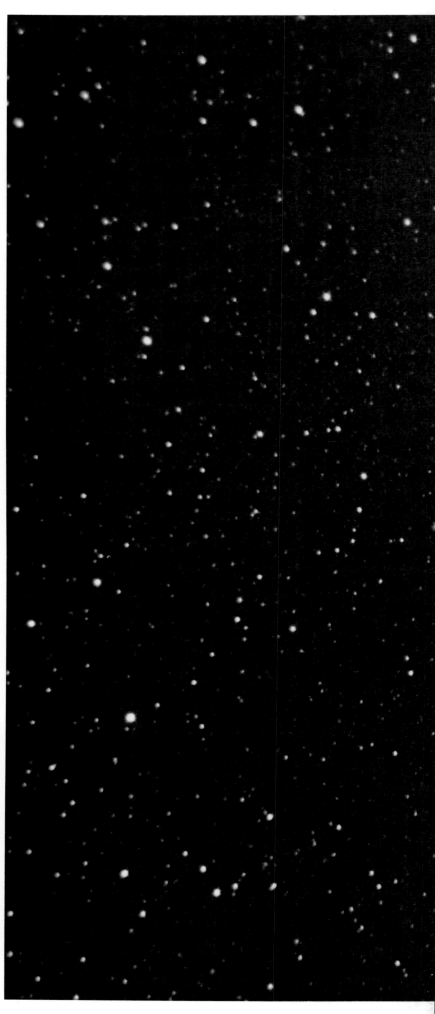

At right: A view of Taurus, a fixed earth sign. *Above* is a detail, showing the Crab Nebula (not to be confused with Cancer) within the constellation.

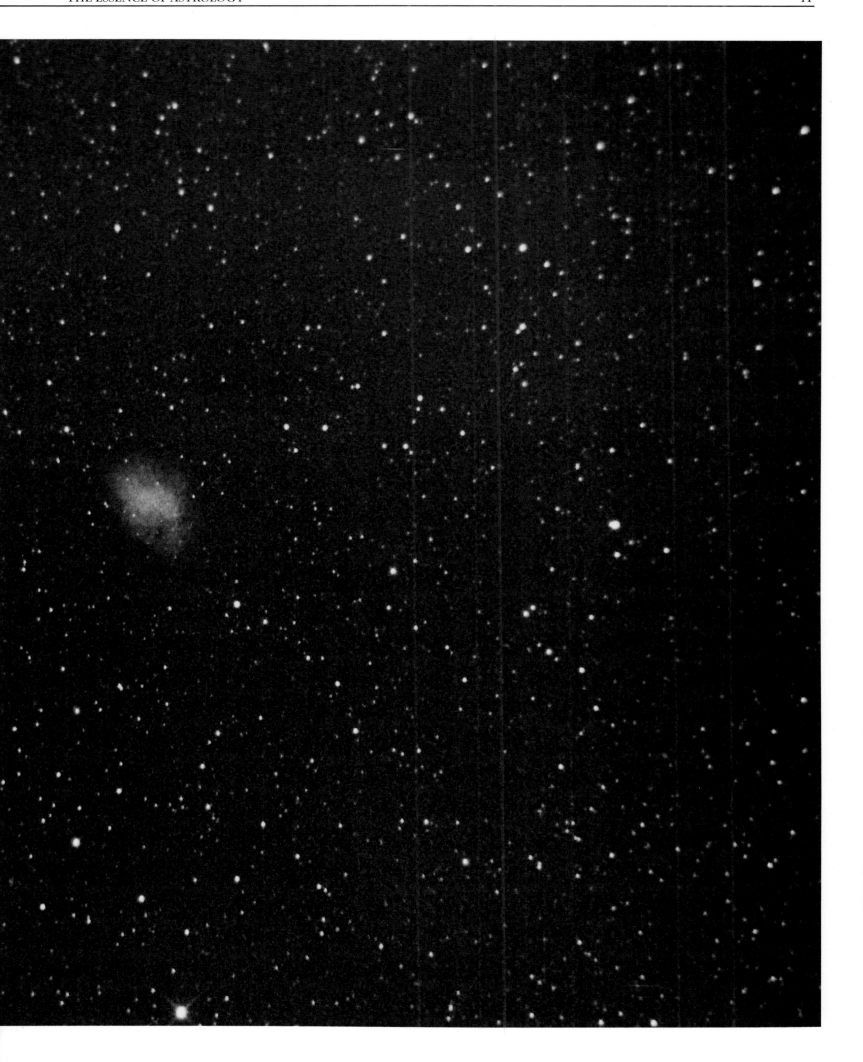

influence of the old persists, but gradually loses its hold day by day, until by the seventh day, the new sign is in full control.

To give fuller interpretation to the signs of the zodiac, they have been divided into periods of approximately 10 days, called the 'decans' or 'decantes,' which cover modifications of individual traits. These are attributed to minor planetary influences, which temper or blend with the ruling influence of the period. A study of these is therefore helpful in forming the individual horoscope, but they are always to be regarded as subordinate to the ruling planet.

Cardinal signs are so called because they are placed at the east, west, north and south points of the astrological figure, hence they compare to the four cardinal points of the compass—the points usually marked by a red arrow. They are variously termed the leading, movable, acute, changeable or initiating signs or types, and as they represent the active temperament, are said to partake of the nature of the ascendant.

Fixed signs are so called because they represent a balance of conflicting forces, are more uniformly referred to as the fixed or grave signs or executive types, although occasionally referred to as the 'foundation' signs—those which most distinctly typify each

The four trinities:

Intellectual (Spring)	Maternal (Summer)	Reproductive (Autumn)	Serving (Winter)
1. Aries	4. Cancer	7. Libra	10. Capricorn
2. Taurus	5. Leo	8. Scorpio	11. Aquarius
3. Gemini	6. Virgo	9. Sagittarius	12. Pisces

Key words associated with the 12 signs:

Aries:	Aspiration	**Libra:**	Equilibrium
Taurus:	Integration	**Scorpio:**	Creativity
Gemini:	Vivification	**Sagittarius:**	Administration
Cancer:	Expansion	**Capricorn:**	Discrimination
Leo:	Assurance	**Aquarius:**	Loyalty
Virgo:	Assimilation	**Pisces:**	Appreciation

At right: **A fiery deep-space view of the constellation Leo, a 'fixed fire sign.'** *Above* **is a detail of same, showing the Spiral Galaxy in Leo.**

element, because of which they were said to have been dominant in the formulation of the Mosaic laws. They have also been called the seismic or 'earthquake' signs, on the assumption that earthquakes most frequently occur when the Sun or Moon is in a fixed sign. They are the powerhouses of the zodiac—reservoirs of energy; the Formators of the Chaldeans, the Cherubim of the Hebrews—the builders of the world. The fixed sign tenacity is depended upon to support or stabilize the leading signs.

Mutable signs, representing the arcs in which there is a perpetual condition of slowing down in readiness to turn a corner; a mobilization for action, and the indecision which results or accompanies it, were symbolized by concepts which would express this duality—the twins, the two deep-water seahorses, or the half-man, half-horse of the Archer; hence also called the dual or the double-bodied signs; and by some, the common or flexed signs. They are the minds of their triplicity, with their quickness and versatility acting as mediators between the leading and fixed signs. They have been called 'the reconcilers of the universe.'

The signs of the zodiac should not be confounded with the zodiac of constellations with which they have only a historic relationship. Somewhat before the Christian era, the constellations and the signs coincided, but since then, the precession (c 25 AD) of the equinoctial point has produced a separation of approximately one degree in 72 years, or a total of about 30 degrees in 2000 years.

Zodiacal aspects are measured in degrees along the Ecliptic. When used in connection with primary directions, the subject's place is taken without latitude, in contrast to the usual method used with mundane aspects, wherein one takes cognizance of the latitude the significator will have when it arrives at the longitudinal degree at which the aspect is complete.

Zodiacal directions are formed in the zodiac by the progressed motion of ascendant, midheaven, sun and moon, to aspects with the planets. These may be: direct, in the order of the signs, or converse, against the order of the signs.

Zodiacal metals as used by alchemists and astrologers:

Aries/Scorpio:	Iron
Taurus/Libra:	Copper
Gemini/Virgo:	Mercury
Cancer:	Silver
Leo:	Gold
Sagittarius/Pisces:	Tin
Capricorn/Aquarius:	Lead

Above: **A closeup of the 'Sombrero Galaxy' that lies in Virgo.** *At right:* **The bright stars of the Pleiades, in the shoulder of Taurus, the bull.**

THE SIGNS OF THE ZODIAC
ARIES
(The Ram)

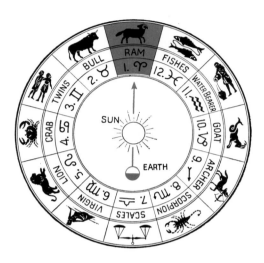

The first sign of the zodiac, Aries' symbol, as shown above, represents the head and horns of the ram. It is a symbol of offensive power—a weapon of the gods, hence an implement of the will. The Babylonians sacrificed rams during the period when the Sun occupied this sign, which occurs annually from 21 March to 20 April. Astrologically and astronomically it is the first 30-degree arc beginning at the point of the Spring Equinox.

According to Greek mythology, Nephele, the mother of Phrixus and Helle, gave her son a ram with a golden fleece. To escape the evil designs of their stepmother, Hera, Phrixus and Helle mounted the ram and fled. As they reached the sea and attempted to cross, Helle fell into the water and perished—hence, the Hellespont. Arriving in Colchis, Phrixus was received by King Aeetes, who sacrificed the ram and dedicated the fleece to Zeus. The golden fleece was later carried away by Jason. Zeus then transported the ram into the heavens as a constellation. (See page 108.)

Aries is the leading quality of the fire element: positive, diurnal, movable, dry, hot, fiery, choleric and violent. Ruled by Mars and exalted by the Sun, Aries in turn exerts its rulership influence over the nations of Britain, Denmark, Germany, Lithuania, Poland and Syria, as well as cities such as Naples, Padua, Zaragosa and Utrecht.

The Aries colors are red and white.

In Aries, Mars doubles its influence, this being its own sign. The Aries nature becomes proportionately strong, with impetuosity its predominant trait. The Sun, combined with Mars, develops the drive found in this sign, urging the individual to great achievements. It also intensifies the Ariean's ideas of right and wrong, often resulting in a crusading spirit that goes beyond normal bounds and defeats its own interests. Saturn with Mars gives Arieans a petulant, impulsive disposition that can hamper the natu-

Above: Comedian Eddie Murphy (3 April 1961) is an Aries. His confrontive wit and his readily pugnacious nature are hallmarks of the Aries character. But why does he have an Aquarius logo on his tie?

Above: Charlie Chaplin (16 April 1889), was known worldwide as the 'Little Tramp' of his comedies—whose often capricious, ill-considered schemes and petulant moods mirrored Aries tendencies.

Above from left: Leonard Nimoy (26 March 1931) and William Shatner (22 March 1931), of *Star Trek*, are both Aries, and exhibit similar facial features. Deforest Kelley is not an Aries, but an Aquarius.

ral foresight of the sign and may lead to unwise speculations. The Moon gives impatience to Mars, resulting in changeable, self-defeating action. Mercury can also make Aries' Mars unfavorable by adding scheming ways to the keen, ambitious Aries nature, thus turning it to selfish interests.

However, Venus, when it combines with Aries' Mars, supplies a kindly quality to the natural drive of Aries, although it does not add the self-control and patience needed in this sign. Jupiter gives purpose to the Aries' Mars, so that this sign also shows true daring and sincere ambition. Conformity to accepted standards is advisable for Arieans in order for them to control their rebellious streak, which they should try to confine to worthy causes.

Though quick to anger, Aries people often calm easily. They are naturally humorous and quick of wit, and enjoy music and entertainment. They say the right thing at the right time, and as students, they are often keen and have the ability of applying whatever they learn to the best advantage.

In business, Arieans are specially suited to being good salespeople, and their drive is valuable in real estate and financial fields. Professionally, they are fine actors, capable lawyers and statesmen. They are also qualified for literary and artistic work.

Due to their strong executive ability, Aries people usually do better on their own, rather than entering into any partnership. However, they need business associates to a degree and their surest choice is someone born under Taurus. While Aries teams well with Sagittarius, Aquarius and Pisces, any of those are apt to profit more from the association unless the Aries person is strongly dominant. Any association between Aries and Capricorn or Aries and Scorpio may prove highly problematic.

In love and marriage, Arieans frequently find harmony and understanding with those born in Leo, Sagittarius or under their own sign. Marriages with Gemini or Libra are regarded as specially suited to the Aries temperament.

Above left: Diana Ross (26 March 1944) exercised the strong Aries solo aspect when she took to the stage on her own, after a stint with the Supremes. *At top, above:* The fiery and petulant Bette Davis' mordant wit reflects the Aries humor. *Above:* Soviet Cosmonaut Yuri Gagarin (9 March 1934), the first man to orbit the Earth, typifies the Aries drive toward achievement. *At right:* Marlon Brando (3 April 1924) has the Aries tendencies toward being an entertainer and being self-contained in an exceptionally strong combination, as exhibited in his 'Method' acting.

THE SIGNS OF THE ZODIAC
TAURUS
(The Bull)

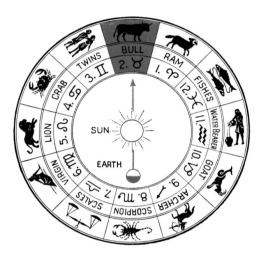

The second sign of the zodiac, Taurus' symbol, as shown in the chart above, represents the head and horns of a bull. The sacred Apis was presumed to be the incarnation of the god Osiris—hence a symbol of a sepulcher or tomb. According to Roman legend, Jupiter, assuming the form of a bull, mingled with the herd when Europa, with whom he was infatuated, and her maidens disported themselves on the seashore. Encouraged by the tameness of the bull, Europa mounted it, whereupon the god rushed into the sea and bore her away to Crete. According to other accounts Taurus represents Io, whom Jupiter turned into a cow in order to deceive Juno. The Sun's entry into Taurus was celebrated as a Feast of Maya (Maia)—our May Day—the Sun represented by a white bull with a golden disc between his horns, followed by a procession of virgins, exemplifying the fecundity of nature in spring.

Taurus as a bull was identified during antiquity as a constellation containing two star clusters—the Pleiades and Hyades—which are referred to in the Old Testament. The principal star of the Hyades, Aldebaran, is mentioned by Hesiod and Homer.

According to the Greeks, Taurus was the bull which carried Europa across the seas to Crete, and which Jupiter raised to the heavens. The Hyades, named Ambrosia, Coronis, Eudora, Pasithoe, Plexaris, Pytho and Tycho—after the seven daughters of Atlas and Aethra—were also transformed into stars by Jupiter for bewailing the death of their brother Hyas.

The central star of the Pleiades is Alcyone, which, like Pleione and Atlas, is a star of the third magnitude. The Pleiades were the seven daughters of Atlas and Pleione, hence half-sisters of the Hyades. They, too, were said to have been turned into stars for grieving over the loss of their sisters and the suffering of their father. Another account tells that after the sisters met the great hunter Orion in Boeotia, his passions were so inflamed at the sight of them that he pursued them through the woods for five years, until Zeus translated the lot of them—the sisters, Orion and his dogs, Sirius and Betelguese—into the sky. (See page 114.)

As the Pleiades rise in mid-May, they are, as daughters of Atlas, the bringer of the fertilizing spring rains which come out of the west. As they set at the end of October, they are, as the pursued of Orion, the forerunners of the autumn storms. It was the Pleiades that Homer, in his *Odyssey* (XII.62), probably alluded to as the doves that brought Ambrosia from the west to Zeus.

That one of the doves was lost while pursuing the wandering rocks, the Planetae, is a reference to the fact that one of the Pleiades, Merope, is always invisible—from hiding her light for shame at having had sexual intercourse with Sisyphus, a mortal. However, all the Pleiades became ancestresses of heroic or divine families, called Vergiliae (probably from *ver*—spring) by the Romans.

The Sun is in Taurus annually from 21 April to 20 May. Astrologically and astronomically it is in the second 30-degree arc from the Spring Equinox, for 30 degrees to 60 degrees along the ecliptic. It is the fixed quality of the Earth element, conferring external will power, which, ordinarily passive and negative, becomes obstinate and unbending when aroused.

In an irony for so masculine an image as a bull, Taurus is ruled by Venus and exalted by the Moon. In turn, Taurus exerts its rulership influence over the nations of Ireland, Iran and the Netherlands, as well as the Soviet republics of Azerbaijan, Byelorussia and Georgia. Cities ruled by Taurus include Dublin, Leipzig, Palermo and St Louis, Missouri.

The colors associated with Taurus are red and citron.

In Taurus, the Sun, combined with Venus, adds great warmth to

Above: William Shakespeare (23 April 1564) was a Taurus born in Aries-influenced England. These influences helped his unprecedented writing career with creativity and strong drive. *Above right:* Likewise, Arthur

Wellesley, Duke of Wellington (1 May 1769) was born in Ireland, which is influenced by Taurus. A very intellectual soldier, his career was capped by decisive victory over Napolean at Waterloo (18 June 1815).

an already friendly nature. It increases the natural strength of this sign, tempering it with honesty and self-control. The Moon further softens an already indulgent nature, but personal gratification and similar faults are apt to retard development.

Mercury decreases the power of Venus, often turning the sympathy of this sign into jealousy and intrigue, but natural abilities are generally quickened, sometimes in a helpful way. The influence of Venus is doubled, producing a sympathetic rather than a stubborn type; but the love of pleasure will be overevident and detrimental. Mars adds strength to Venus, and also increases the sensual, pleasure-loving trend of this sign, without counteracting undesirable traits.

In Taurus, Jupiter and Venus are very favorable. Strength is added to all the good traits of this sign, and obstinate, pleasure-loving trends are overcome. Meanwhile, Saturn with Venus adds intellectuality, but may increase the obstinate disposition of this sign. This can result in extremes of self-gratification.

Strength is the predominating feature of this sign. With it, however, there is a stubborn, firm-set nature that is difficult to change. The governing planet, Venus, emotional and fraught with primitive urges, furthers these Taurian trends rather than repressing them.

In business, the practical mind of Taurus is suited to constructive fields. They can succeed in all mechanical lines, as engineers, builders and contractors. Often mathematical-minded, they are capable cashiers and accountants. Here, their trustworthy nature, once recognized, may raise them to high position in financial circles. They are good teachers, due to their natural sympathy. Their artistic ability is often on the practical side, producing photographers and landscape architects.

In partnerships, Taurus persons do well with those born under Aries or Gemini. An Aries partner can supply the initial drive for an endeavor which the Taurus individual then shoulders the responsibility to move forward. From a Gemini individual, a Taurian will gain a variety of ideas, some of which are sure to be suited to the practical mind of Taurus. Good business associations for Taurus are frequently found with Scorpio, Capricorn or Pisces.

In love and marriage, Taurus and Scorpio often prove ideal, each being strong or forceful, while supplying qualities that the other needs. Taurus and Virgo are well suited because of the latter's analytical ability. Taurus may do well with Libra, who adds good judgment to the union, but there is often an element of uncertainty here. Taurus and Capricorn are a very fine marital combination.

Above: Shirley MacLaine (24 April 1934) is one of the most recognizable of current stars, and is also one of the leading figures in the New Age movement. Her insistence on the propriety of New Age doctrine, despite her many detractors, is a typical Taurean tenacity—in itself a useful tool, depending on circumstances.

MacLaine's co-star in *Terms of Endearment* was Jack Nicholson (22

April 1937) *(above right).* Both MacLaine and Nicholson love the spotlight, exhibiting a steady, almost myopic ability to project their strong personalities into whatever role they play. *At right:* Great Britain's Queen Elizabeth II (21 March 1926) is typically calm and steady, with the deep strength it takes to be one of the world's leading public figures. Prince Phillip (10 June 1921), her husband, was born under the sign of Gemini.

THE SIGNS OF THE ZODIAC
GEMINI
(The Twins)

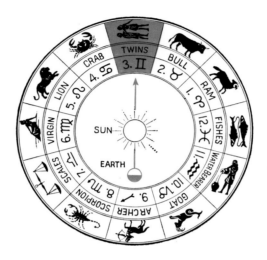

The third sign of the zodiac, Gemini's symbol, as indicated in the chart above, represents two pieces of wood bound together, symbolic of the unremitting conflict of contradictory mental processes.

The constellation Gemini contains Castor and Pollux, the Dioscuri, twin sons of Jupiter and Leda, associated with Romulus and Remus, who were the founders of Rome. The constellation Lupus represents the wolf by whom the twins were suckled in infancy. In other references the twins are identified as Hercules and Apollo, and as Triptolemus and Iasion. The Arabians depicted the twins as a pair of peacocks. (See page 110.)

The Sun is in Gemini annually from 21 May to 20 June. Astrologically it is the 30-degree arc immediately preceding the Summer Solstice, marked by the passing of the Sun over the Tropic of Cancer, and occupying a position along the ecliptic from 60 degrees to 90 degrees. It is the mutable quality of the element: positive, dual.

Ruled by Mercury, this schizoid Sun sign in turn exerts its ruling influence over the nations of Belgium, the Sudan and United States, as well as Britain's west country, the Soviet republic of Armenia and the Italian island of Sardinia. Cities ruled by the sign of the twins include London, Louvain, Nuremburg and Versailles.

The Gemini colors—two, of course—are red and white.

In Gemini, the Sun develops the favorable side of Mercury, adding power of concentration and generally inducing the native of Gemini to turn his versatility to good use. Great eloquence and striking personality may result from this combination.

The Moon hinders the favorable aspects of Mercury. This produces a temperament that is always on the jump, never taking time to develop a given talent. The Moon, however, does make the mind

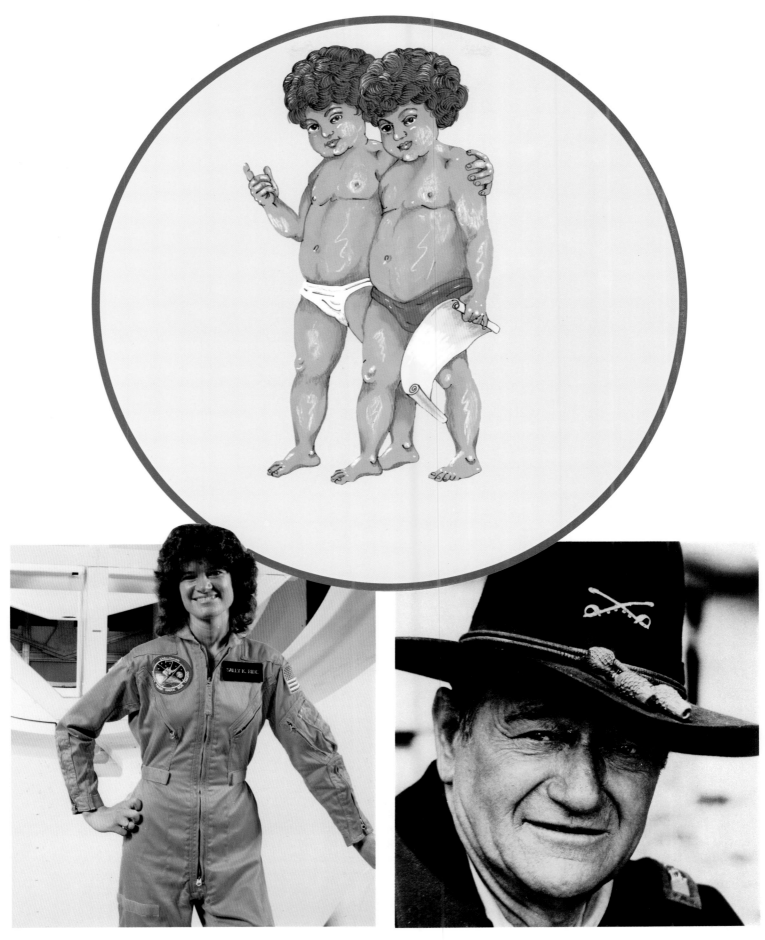

At left: Singer and actress Cher (born Cherilyn LaPiere on 20 May 1946), is often noted for the enthusiasm of her approach to show business, as well as her acting ability. *Above:* Astronaut Dr Sally K Ride (26 May 1951), the first American woman in space, embodies the 'I can do anything' aspect of the multi-talented Gemini influence. *Above right:* Arguably one of the most self-assured, commanding screen presences of the past half-century was John Wayne (26 May 1907), whose combination of solid strength and unexpected tenderness was a hallmark of Wild West films.

receptive, and its influence fades in the face of stronger indications.

In Gemini, Mercury accentuates all the characteristics of its own sign. This can be very dangerous unless modified by lesser influences. Together with Venus, Mercury adds to the superficial trend of this sign. Things of the moment tend to prevail, and persons of this type will use sentiment to further their own desires.

Mars adds drive to Mercury, increasing the unfortunate aspects of this sign. The Gemini nature, already active, can become violent and sometimes unpredictable. Jupiter, though, provides Mercury with a frank, direct approach, which is helpful to this often unpredictable sign. Saturn and Mercury together can develop the mentality of Gemini to the point of real genius, but this can prove harmful when such inventive talent is diverted to unscrupulous purposes, resulting in a very dangerous combination.

A duality of nature is a concomitant of the Twin sign, and while cases of split personality are comparatively rare, the Gemini mind runs to contradictions. Gemini people have a way of going from hot to cold, like the swing of a pendulum. Their friendly attitude may shift to mistrust when they encounter problems. They are often unconventional as well as skeptical, and their keen foresight may suffer through overenthusiasm, causing them to let real opportunities languish while they go after something else. Above all, Geminis should never waste what they have gained, for though they picture each success as building to something bigger, they may overlook the obstacles that can ruin such hopes.

Being born under not just one lucky star but two, Gemini people should make the most of opportunities while they can, remembering that even 'double luck' can run out and result in nothing.

In business, Gemini people fit almost anywhere. They are good salespeople, promoters and often successful speculators. They do well in advertising, publishing, television, transportation and other fields where they must keep up with trends. They do well with Taurus, for persons of that sign are receptive to Gemini notions and will see them through to completion. The balanced nature of Libra and the straight-aiming qualities of Sagittarius make both of these signs good partners for those born under Gemini. One of the strongest combinations in the zodiac is that of a versatile Gemini and a conservative Cancer, provided the latter serves strictly as a counter-balance rather than a drag.

In love and marriage, Gemini and Libra are well suited, as are Gemini and Aquarius. But some restraining force is needed, due to the wavering natures in both cases. Gemini gains drive from an Aries marriage and exuberance from a mate born under Leo. Gemini and Sagittarius form an unusually good marital combination.

For some, it is astonishing that three such diverse personalities as US President John F Kennedy (29 May 1917) *(above right)*; actress Marilyn Monroe (1 June 1926) *(above left)*; and 'dean of actors' Sir Laurence Olivier (22 May 1907) *(above)* were born under the same astrological sign.

Add to this legendary pop singer Bob Dylan (24 May 1941) *(at right)*; actor Michael J Fox (9 June 1961) *(right center)*; and Sir Arthur Conan Doyle (22 May 1859) *(far right)* and the diversity leans toward the arts.

An entry not to be left off the list when considering those born under Gemini is England's great Queen Victoria (24 May 1819) *(above right)*.

THE SIGNS OF THE ZODIAC
CANCER
(The Crab)

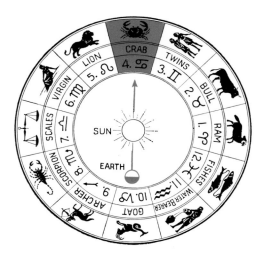

T he fourth sign of the zodiac, Cancer's symbol, which is shown in the chart above, is presumed to represent the folded claws of a crab, is thought by Nicholas DeVore to symbolize the joining together of a male and female essence, as indicative of the most maternal of all the signs.

Cancer is named for a loose cluster of stars, with Praesepe, the 'beehive nebula,' visible to the naked eye as a nebulous patch. Roman legend holds that Cancer is the crab that bit Hercules during his fight with the Lernean Hydra, and it was placed amongst the stars in gratitude by Juno, the enemy of Hercules. Aratus mentions Cancer in the third century BC, and Ptolemy catalogued 13 stars within the area, although none are brighter than the third magnitude. The *Encyclopedia Britannica* explains the name as possibly due to the fact that, at this point, the Sun, passing the location of its greatest elongation, apparently retraces its path in a sidelong manner resembling the movements of a crab. (See page 108.) In Egyptian astrology, Cancer is represented by the scarab.

The Sun is in Cancer annually from 21 June to 22 July. Astrologically and astronomically it is the first 30-degree arc following the Summer Solstice, marked by the Sun's passing of the Tropic of Cancer, and occupying a position along the ecliptic from 90 degrees to 120 degrees. It represents the leading qualities of the water element, being negative, cold, moist, phlegmatic, nocturnal, commanding, movable, fruitful, weak, unfortunate, crooked and mute.

Cancerians are ruled by the Moon and, in fact, are occasionally referred to in literature as 'Moon children.' This sign in turn exerts its rulership over Scotland and western Africa, as well as an unusually large number of cities, which include Amsterdam, Berne, Cadiz, Genoa, Istanbul, Manchester, Milan, New York, Stockholm, Tunis, Venice and York.

These pages, left to right: Meryl Streep, Harrison Ford and Louis Armstrong all demonstrate the creative, yet traditional side of Cancer. Streep is a fine actress whose emotional nuances give added depth to her roles; Ford's characterizations hearken back to the heroes of adventure films in the 1930s and 1940s. Louis Armstrong broke new ground in jazz improvisation, while still retaining a recognizable melody line. All three found their niche as veritable mainstays of their form of creativity, and yet there is the air of unspoken reserve about each of them.

Cancer's primary color affiliation is green.

In Cancer, which is the Moon's own sign, the lunar influence is doubly strong, but often works on the principle of 'two negatives make a positive,' thus bringing out all the better qualities of the sign. In cooperation with that lunar influence, the Sun produces a highly variable combination of brilliancy and restlessness. The Sun curbs the imaginative disposition of this period, but generally strengthens any good traits. With this influence, Mercury also produces a quickening of the sign's natural traits, but often to disadvantage, as excessive action can defeat receptivity and result in an incompetent, unreliable nature. Though people of this sign are seldom schemers, they may be swayed and used by others. Venus increases the emotional uncertainty of this sign, but the Cancer's natural loyalty and home-loving qualities turn this into a steadying factor. Mars dominates the weaker Moon, arousing action, which can be used to good advantage, but only if controlled. Otherwise, this combination can prove very dangerous. Jupiter steadies the Moon, adding to the dignity of this sign and guiding the conservative, uncertain Cancerian nature towards constructive purposes. When Saturn combines with the Moon, it is seldom helpful, as restlessness, uncertainty and moodiness are accentuated and need other planetary influences to temper them.

Cancerians cling to tradition, yet their moods—and even their purposes—may become as changeable as the Moon itself. This self-contradiction is understandable, when recognized as part of the individual's innate nature. These people are home centered, and are fond of family life and domestic tranquillity, but they also enjoy travel and adventure. Cancerians have strong determination and great perserverance; otherwise they would not go to the extremes that they do. So, despite some seemingly contradictory characteristics, Cancer can be developed into one of the best of signs by persons who subordinate the morbid side and refuse to dwell in the past.

In business, people of this sign succeed along established lines. They do well as manufacturers and merchants, for with them, quality is important and they take pride in what they produce. However, they must learn to be aggressive. Otherwise they can vacillate and find themselves left far behind.

Cancer and Capricorn are opposite enough to form a strong combination, and there is an affinity between Cancer and Aquarius that also marks them as good business partners. An association with Gemini is excellent, if the Cancer individual can keep his versatile partner under appropriate restraint. In contrast, a teaming with the exuberant Leo is very effective, provided Leo is allowed to dominate in the matter of decisions.

Professionally, they are good teachers, librarians, historians and scientists. They are capable lawyers and politicians. Many Cancerians rise to a high rank in art, literature and music.

In love and marriage, the home-loving nature of Cancer is a highly important factor, but it must be remembered that Cancer mates can suffer through neglect. As in business, Cancer and Capricorn are usually admirably suited to matrimony. Cancer and Pisces are a good combination; while Scorpio and Libra also mate well with Cancer.

Cancers in the UK's Royal Family: *Above left:* **Princess Diana (1 July 1961) and young Prince William (21 June 1982) as well as King Edward VIII (*above*) (23 June 1894) were all born under the sign of the crab. Diana excels at meeting the public and providing a deft domestic touch. Her husband, Prince Charles, is a Scorpio.**

Another typically proficient and responsible Cancer is the comedian Bill Cosby (12 July 1937) (*at right*). His unique—and oblique—sense of humor and acute business acumen has made him one of the world's wealthiest entertainers, and his interest in the community at large has led him to participate in numerous well-established social causes. One of the predominant Cancer qualities is 'hidden strength.'

THE SIGNS OF THE ZODIAC
LEO
(The Lion)

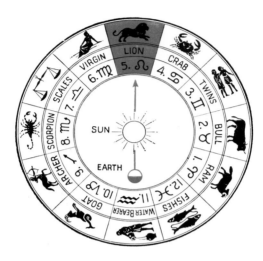

The fourth sign of the zodiac, Leo's symbol, seen above, is possibly an emblem representing the phallus, and was used in ancient Dionysian mysteries. It is also an emblem of the Sun's fire, heat or creative energy.

The constellation Leo is the Nemean lion, slain by Hercules and raised to the heavens in his honor by Zeus. Regulus, the Lion's Heart (also known as Basilicus), is its brightest star with a magnitude of 1.23. The Leonids are a meteoric swarm which radiate from the area, appearing in November of each year. (See page 110.)

The Sun is in Leo annually from 23 July to 22 August. Astrologically and astronomically it is the second 30-degree arc after the Summer Solstice, marked by the Sun's passing of the Tropic of Cancer and occupying a position along the ecliptic from 120 degrees to 150 degrees. It is the fixed quality of the fire element, conferring an internal will motivated by an impulse of the heart. It is positive, hot, dry, choleric, eastern, diurnal, commanding, brutish, sterile, broken, changeable, fortunate, strong, hoarse, bitter and violent.

Ruled, of course, by the Sun itself, Leo exerts its influence over the Bohemia, France and Italy (including Sicily but not Sardinia), as well as the war-torn southern coast of Lebanon and the ancient lands of Cappadocia and Chaldea—where the art of astrology itself was born. Cities ruled by the sign of the Sun include Bath, Bombay, Bristol, Chicago, Damascus, Detroit, Miami, Portsmouth, Prague and the eternal city of Rome.

Leo's colors are, predictably, red or gold.

In Leo, the Sun doubles its power, as this is its own sign. Although this is a very fortunate period with good traits predominant, this sign is sometimes subject to overzeal. Early brilliancy may fail to mature, though fame is often attained.

In Leo, the Moon can have little effect upon the Sun. It gives an individual a hesitant, uncertain trend, but the Leo nature usually

At left: Alfred Hitchcock (13 August 1899) was an autocratic director, and with his eccentric approach to cinematography and plotting, garnered a unique place in the annals of film. *Above left:* Rock star Mick Jagger (26 July 1944), with his stage antics and catlike howls seems to manifest a very catlike nature indeed. Jackie Onassis (28 July 1929) is a notably strong personality, renowned especially for the nobility she exhibited in bearing the death of her first and second husbands—US President John F Kennedy (see Gemini) and Aristotle Onassis (15 January 1906), a Capricorn.

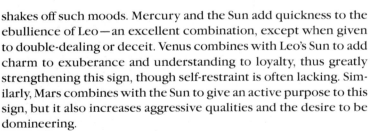

shakes off such moods. Mercury and the Sun add quickness to the ebullience of Leo—an excellent combination, except when given to double-dealing or deceit. Venus combines with Leo's Sun to add charm to exuberance and understanding to loyalty, thus greatly strengthening this sign, though self-restraint is often lacking. Similarly, Mars combines with the Sun to give an active purpose to this sign, but it also increases aggressive qualities and the desire to be domineering.

Jupiter and the Sun are a very fine combination. Jupiter supplies dignity and idealism to the enthusiastic qualities of this sign, with tremendous prospects of success and esteem. Saturn combines with the Sun to give wisdom to idealism, but often retards the fervent nature of this sign, producing periods of gloom and dissatisfaction.

Both ambition and idealism are present under Leo, for the brilliance of this sign reflects the grandeur of its governing planet, the Sun. But Leo, as well as being high-minded, can be high-handed. When people of this type fall victim to their own short-comings, the result can prove disastrous. There is little of the negative in this sign, and Leo people are most often impulsive, generous and brave, and quick to follow their own intuition. Their success is furthered by their marked influence upon all they meet, and and they often win over those who oppose them by the sheer force of their magnetic personalities.

Leos love the spotlight, perhaps because to them it is the Sun in miniature. They insist upon charting their own course and do so with an inherent vigor. They override their own faults so naturally that they often are not even aware of them.

Leo people enjoy everything that is active, including outdoor life, for they crave the warmth of the Sun that is so predominant in their sign. Indolence is the greatest of drawbacks to the Leo temperament. Leos will revel in ease and luxury until they are forced to action, either through necessity or their own self-imposed demands.

In business, Leo offers unlimited prospects. Along strictly com-mercial lines, Leo people star in special fields. Anything requiring promotion or enthusiastic development falls in the Leo's domain. Thus, Leos make capable hotel managers, restauranteurs, real estate developers, publishers and executives, for their spirit is contagious. As partners, they team well with persons of all signs, but do particularly well with those born under Cancer, Virgo and Aquarius.

Leos also succeed in many professions because they have a flair for showmanship, which can sway clients just as effectively as audiences. Many noted actors were born under this sign, and, in the literary field, they have had a strong trend toward the dra-matic—all part of the Leo makeup.

In love and marriage, the Leo exuberance is also generally helpful, though not always harmonious. Leos are perhaps best suited to Aries, Sagittarius or Aquarius, but they also have excel-lent marital prospects with Cancer and Virgo, as well as those of their own sign.

Above left: **Napolean Bonaparte (15 August 1769) at the Battle of Arcola, November 1796. Napolean, a brilliant general fell to defeat at Waterloo on 18 June 1815 (see Duke of Wellington, Taurus). His overreliance on his own intuitions gave the allied British and Prussian forces just the edge they needed.** *Above:* **Pop singer and exhibitionist Madonna is a Leo, and manifests an intense pride in her own sensibilities.** *At right:* **Mae West (17 August 1892) had many of the same traits as director Alfred Hitchcock. Both were interested in projecting a wholly individualistic viewpoint, and both were autocratic in their approach to the production of films.**

THE SIGNS OF THE ZODIAC
VIRGO
(The Virgin)

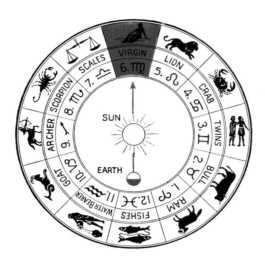

The sixth sign of the zodiac, Virgo's symbol, shown above as a modified 'M,' is probably a reference to the immaculate conception of a messiah. Virgo is usually depicted as a virgin holding in her hand a green branch, an ear of corn or a spike of grain. Spica, a star of the first magnitude, with a very faint companion, is the principal star in the constellation of Virgo. This star is named for the city where the Festival of Ishtar, goddess of fertility, was celebrated.

According to different fables, Virgo is modeled after Justitia, daughter of Astraeus and Ancora, who lived before man sinned, and taught him his duty. At the end of the golden age she returned to her place in the heavens. Hesiod identified her as the daughter of Jupiter and Themis. Others variously identify her as Erigone, daughter of Icarius, and Parthene, daughter of Apollo. (See page 116.)

The Sun is in Virgo annually from 23 August to 22 September. Astrologically and astronomically it is the 30-degree arc immediately preceding the Sun's passing over the Fall Equinoctial point, occupying a position along the ecliptic from 150 degrees to 180 degrees. It is the mutable quality of the Earth element: negative, cold, dry, sterile and human, and also critical, practical and helpful.

Ruled by swift, sure Mercury, Virgo in turn casts its influence over the regions of the Middle East which were pivotal centers of the birth of our civilization, such as Assyria, Babylon, Candia, Corinth, Crete, Croatia, Mesopotamia and Thessalonia. Modern Turkey is, of course, also included, as is modern day Switzerland. Cities ruled by the Virgin's stars include the ancient cities of Bagdad and Jerusalem, as well as Basel, Boston, Heidelburg, Lyon, Paris, Reading (England) and Washington, DC.

The Virgo color is, as one might expect, the white of driven

At left: Legendary actress Greta Garbo (18 September 1905) had the quiet, musing air of the sometimes secretive Virgo sign. *Above:* Actress Lauren Bacall (16 September 1924) often played characters who were uncommonly acute, and were memorably played opposite her husband, Humphrey Bogart (23 January 1899)—a straight-talking Aquarius—in such films as *The Big Sleep.* Italian actress Sophia Loren (20 September 1934) *(above right)* often exercised the strong Virgo aptitude for expressing scorn, in her roles as women in difficult circumstances trying to keep their dignity.

snow, although some scholars, such as Nicholas DeVore, describe the color as 'black with blue splotches.'

In Virgo, the Sun combined with Mercury puts power of analysis to good use, with great results if applied to important aims. However, wasted talent can result through overinvolvement with trivial detail or too much self-pride.

The Moon also combines well with Mercury. Here, its receptive quality is a great adjunct to the Virgo ability of analysis, enabling Virgos to apply their talents in innovative ways. Its danger is an overactive imagination, which may lead to constant worry.

This being Mercury's sign, it has double strength, which increases Virgo's cleverness and analytical ability while lessening the quality of imagination. However, scheming tendencies must be curbed, as they are very marked under this double influence.

Venus adds creative artistry to the skill of Virgo. This combination brings friendliness and understanding to the Virgo temperament, and, although it is generally good, can possibly result in wasted effort. Mars is also usually favorable, as Mars adds action to the logical nature of Virgo. Dubious projects should be avoided.

Jupiter helps Mercury, causing the keen Virgo mind to seek high callings and honorable professions in which the skill of this sign functions to the fullest. Integrity must be maintained, however, or persons with this combination may become shallow and superficial. Saturn combines with Mercury to turn the intellectual ability of Virgos into skeptical channels. People under such influence become argumentative, applying their knowledge to useless—and sometimes base—purposes. Other mitigating influences are needed.

Virgo people have inquiring minds that will not rest until they have learned all they want to know about a subject. They are skilled at drawing information from people, then filling in from other sources or rationalizing facts into a complete and remarkably accurate picture. Often they pick up essential data without anyone realizing what they are about. Along with keen analysis, they have exceptional memories; otherwise, they could not form the exact comparisons that they do.

Order and harmony are essential to the Virgo mind. Therefore, Virgo people should simplify their lives and purposes, or they will bog down under a mass of detail that their exacting minds cannot ignore. The less little things to bother them, the greater their capacity for higher aims. Virgo people are usually tolerant, but once blind to their own faults, they may become even more opinionated than those whom they criticize.

Imagination rules the Virgo mind, making them fearful of accidents, illness and financial problems. They are sensitive to pain and any kind of suffering, which makes them superficially sympathetic to those who experience misfortune.

In business, Virgo people are suited to special lines, where their quick minds see new opportunities or productive deals. They are good at evaluating business conditions and market trends. They become good writers, editors, lawyers and professors because they size up things quickly and apply their conclusions ingeniously. Many become architects or designers. However, as actors, lecturers and performers they must overcome their self-consciousness to succeed, and the same often applies in sales.

Where a business partnership is concerned, Virgo's analytical ability teams well with Leo's exuberance. Virgo also gains much from Libra's judgment and intuition, but here, Virgo may chafe under restraint. This sign also does well with Pisces, and sometimes Scorpio. In fact, Virgos get along in business with nearly every other sign, but others are apt to gain far more from the Virgo than they give in return. Therefore, Virgos must be very careful in their choice of business associates.

Love and marriage present problems for Virgos because of the exacting, fault-finding and sometimes demanding nature evidenced by this sign. One of the best marital combinations for Virgo is with another of the same sign, as each may understand the other's critical moods. Virgos may find happiness with those born under the sign of Pisces, while Aries, Taurus and Capricorn would also prove compatible. Virgo and Libra could be helpful to each other, but their strong minds might too often come in conflict, making this a dubious union.

Above far left: Sean Connery (25 August 1930) evinced sharp-minded calculation in the James Bond movie thrillers. *Above middle:* Peter Sellers (8 September 1925) displayed a deceptive naivete in the ludicrous *Pink Panther* films, and as Chance, the gardener, in *Being There*.

Larry Hagman (21 September 1931) displayed the marked Virgo tendency for subtle schemes and plots in his role as JR Ewing in the television series *Dallas* (in which he starred opposite Linda Gray who is also a Virgo). *At right:* The legendary Ingrid Bergman (29 August 1913) made an acting trademark of restraint, and was notably aloof in her personal life.

THE SIGNS OF THE ZODIAC
LIBRA
(The Scales)

The seventh sign of the zodiac, Libra's symmetrical symbol, seen in the chart above, represents the balancing scales, and, as such, is emblematic of equilibrium and justice.

Libra, the constellation, was first mentioned by Manetho in the third century BC and later by Germinus in the first century BC. Prior to that time, Libra was not considered an independent constellation, but rather as Chelae, the claws of Scorpio. Although it was not cited by Aratus, Ptolemy catalogued 17 stars in the area. Libra contains the important star Algol, a variable, whose magnitude ranges from 5 to 6.2, with a period of 56 hours, 51 minutes. The *Encyclopedia Britannica* gives no explanation for the name beyond the fact that there the days and nights are of equal duration, which would also apply to Aries. (See page 112.)

The Sun is in Libra annually from 23 September to 22 October. Astrologically and astronomically it is the first 30-degree arc following the passing of the Sun over the Fall Equinoctial point, occupying a position along the ecliptic from 180 degrees to 210 degrees. It is the leading quality of the air element, characterized by being positive, hot, moist, sweet, obeying, restless and judicial.

Ruled by Venus and exalted by Saturn, Libra rules many widespread nations of the Earth, including Argentina, Austria, Burma, China, Egypt, Japan and Tibet, as well as such cities as Antwerp, Lisbon and Vienna.

Libra's colors range from dark crimson to black.

In Libra, the Sun steadies the temperamental side of Venus, stressing fair judgment and providing originality, thus making Librans the most likable of people. However, overconfidence may produce strongly formed opinions, which often should be avoided.

The Moon combines unfavorably with Venus. Natural sympathy is stimulated, producing the kindliest of natures, but there is a

What some felt to be an all-too-even-handed approach to his office was suddenly and tragically dispensed with in the midnight helicopter raid on Iran: US President Jimmy Carter (1 October 1924) *(at left)* was generally a 'moderate's moderate.' Leading French film star Yves Mon-

tand (13 October 1921) *(above left)* began as a singer, and has co-starred in several film vehicles with his wife, Simone Signoret (25 March 1921), an Aries. French film star Catherine Deneuve (22 October 1943) *(above right)* here shows the balanced but penetrating Libra expression.

craving for excitement, acceptance of new fads and a generally careless disposition.

Venus exerts a double influence on this sign, increasing the traits of Virgo to an exaggerated extent. Good or bad, sink or swim, is the indication here, depending on the individual and which traits he or she develops. Mars unites with Venus to add strength and activity to this sign, but it may also narrow many purposes at the expense of fair judgment, reducing the naturally sympathetic nature of the Libran.

Jupiter adds strength to Libra's Venus, confining the judgment of this sign to important affairs and turning the affections and sympathies of Libra to worthy persons and commendable causes. On the other hand, Saturn with Venus can hamper the good judgment of this sign, often changing sympathy to jealousy. Thus, much effort is needed to counteract this tendency.

Everything in Libra has to do with balance; hence the susceptibility of the Libra individual is counterbalanced by a strong-mindedness that can become firm and unflinching in purpose. Libra is the sign of justice, and indicative of persons who balance everything to a nicety, always trying to promote good will and friendship, even if they must go to extremes to do so. This is actuated by their inherent love of harmony and beauty, as reflected by the beneficial gleam of Venus.

Intuition is a guiding force with Librans and often enables them to ferret out deceit and insincerity, no matter how much it is glossed over. However, if they prejudge a matter, or listen to persons in whom they trust or sympathize, Librans can be carried far astray. They are so vulnerable to the influence of those who impress them that they will imitate the manners of such persons and actually pick up their traits.

Compassion and understanding are paramount with Librans. They are never deaf to an appeal from family or friends and they will often champion the underdog, if they seem to represent a deserving cause, even against their sounder judgment. Such is their need to equalize matters and produce harmony.

In business, Libra people often rise to high positions, as their judgment, when properly exercised, is of the executive type. Similarly, their understanding toward subordinates can prove a powerful asset. Their intuitive ability makes them excellent merchants and their hunches aid them in speculative fields. However, they should curb their gambling instinct or it may run away with them. Yet, at the same time, such an instinct can serve as an asset in certain fields.

Libra people often become inventors, researchers or historians.

Their talent to play a part makes them fine actors, and they are excellent musicians and singers as well. They are also mathematically minded and are suited to many arts and crafts. Since Librans rely on their own judgment, they should be wary of business partnerships. They team well with Gemini, Virgo or Scorpio, provided they agree to rely on the Libra's judgment. Many other signs, especially Pisces, are too cautious to team up with Librans.

In love and marriage, Libra does well with Aries because of the latter's drive. Libra gains animation from marriage with Leo. Perhaps the susceptible Libra and jovial Sagittarius are the best mating of all, but Libra also harmonizes with Aquarius and can benefit from a pairing with Gemini or Scorpio. There is a natural attraction between Libra and Virgo, but conflicts of interests may result, and Libra and Pisces are seldom a suitable combination.

Above: Actress Lillian Gish (14 October 1896) gave what Pauline Kael called 'one of the most beautifully sustained performances in screen history' as Hester Prynne in the film adaptation of Nathaniel Hawthorne's *The Scarlet Letter. Above left:* British Prime Minister Margaret Thatcher (13 October 1925), a Libra, and Queen Elizabeth II (21 April 1926), a Taurus, have been a remarkable combination for the United Kingdom.

Rock and roll star Jerry Lee Lewis (29 September 1935) *(above center)* exhibits an extremely adventursome side that could be said to be 'easily led' into disaster. *Above right:* Rock star Sting (born Matthew Gordon Sumner on 2 October 1951) has that typically questioning Libra look. *At right:* One of the most susceptible, imaginative performers: John Lennon (9 October 1940).

THE SIGNS OF THE ZODIAC
SCORPIO
(The Scorpion)

The eighth sign of the zodiac, Scorpio's symbol, as shown above, resembles that of Virgo, but with an arrow on the tail—doubtless to represent the sting. It is symbolized by the asp or serpent, harking back to the serpent of the Garden of Eden, and indicating that the will governs, or is governed by, the reproductive urge. It is sometimes symbolized by the dragon, and is frequently linked with the constellation Aquilla, the Eagle.

According to a Greek myth, Orion boasted to Diana and Latona that he would kill every animal on the Earth, whereupon the goddesses sent a scorpion, which stung *him* to death. Jupiter then raised the scorpion to the heavens, but later, at the request of Diana, he also raised Orion. (See page 114.)

The chief star of the constellation Scorpio is Antares, a reddish star of the first magnitude, which has a green companion of the seventh magnitude.

The Sun is in Scorpio annually from 23 October to 22 November. Astrologically and astronomically it is the second 30-degree arc after the Sun's passing of the Fall Equinox, occupying a position along the ecliptic from 210 degrees to 240 degrees. It possesses the fixed quality of the water element, being negative, nocturnal, cold, moist, watery, mute and phlegmatic.

Ruled by Mars, and exalted by Uranus, Scorpio in turn rules Bavaria and Norway, as well as the entirety of northwestern Africa, such as Morocco, Algeria—the old Barbary Coast. Scorpio also rules Ghent and the colorful port cities of Liverpool, Messina and New Orleans.

Scorpio's characteristic color is dark brown.

In Scorpio, the Sun with Mars produces dignity and adds exuberance to the natural energy and determination of this sign. It promises great success, but tends toward arrogance. Under this sign, the Martian influence is definitely doubled, producing con-

Far left: US President Theodore Roosevelt (27 October 1858) coined the slogan 'Speak softly and carry a big stick.' It could well serve as a motto for all born under the sign of Scorpio. Marie Antoinette (2 November 1755) *(above left)*—slain during the Reign of Terror during the French Revolution—made the famous statement 'Let them eat cake,' less out of Scorpio hauteur than from her own experience—after all, when *she* ran out of bread, that's what her household did. *Above right:* Katherine Hepburn's (9 November 1907) stately demeanor has served her acting well.

ceit and forcefulness at the expense of all else—definitely a dangerous combination.

With Mars, the Moon curbs the Scorpion trend towards overdominance, making the individual receptive and therefore more understanding. But it also weakens the urge for action, causing hesitation when drive is needed.

Mercury and Mars are a bad combination, developing the negative and unscrupulous aspects of this sign. Self-control is strong, but is often used to further self-interest. Other planetary influences are needed to modify this combination. Venus, for instance, gives an amorous ardor to this sign, intensifying the desire for pleasure, and natural Venusian sympathy can temper the harsh Scorpio nature.

Jupiter adds integrity and compassion to Scorpio, but does not restrain the boldness of this sign. So, too, is Saturn often helpful to Scorpio, endowing courage with wisdom and adding intellectuality to drive. However, any gloom or cynicism may bring out the faults of Scorpio.

That noted Scorpio, Theodore Roosevelt, was fond of the slogan, 'Speak softly and carry a big stick,' a phrase which aptly sums up the characteristics of this sign. Scorpio people are quiet, even secretive, in manner, yet highly observant. Once roused to action, they are determined, aggressive and dominant, always ready to champion a cause. When they work for the good of others, they rise to great heights and are much respected. But Scorpio people, always well-satisfied with themselves, can easily become domineering and condescending.

Scorpios are blunt, argumentative and natural fighters, and their coolness under fire deceives the opposition and adds to their strength. In the showdown, Scorpio is apt to have the upper hand. They should control their tempers, as well as their actions.

In business, a powerful Scorpio personality can succeed in practically any line. They range from managers of branch offices to the heads of large companies. They have the greatest of opportunities in the expanding world of today, for as heads of bureaus, committees and other investigative groups, no other sign can begin to equal them. Professionally, those born under the sign of Scorpio frequently become great physicians.

In partnership, Scorpio's best choice is Libra, for the bold projects of the Scorpio mind will be weighed and certified by Libra's judgment. Scorpio sometimes does well with Sagittarius, if they can solve the question of togetherness. Virgo, Taurus and Cancer do well with Scorpio, if needed. Always remember that Scorpio can do quite well alone.

In love and marriage, Scorpio finds three strong choices: Taurus, Cancer and Pisces. Scorpio's crusading spirit is admirably seconded by Taurus. The Scorpio boldness carries along the wavering Cancer disposition and brings the strong point of Pisces to the fore. Scorpio may also find a harmonious marriage with Virgo, while Scorpio's power and Leo's exuberance may prove a satisfactory marital combination.

Scorpios can have impressive physical features, as is witnessed by the beauty of Grace Kelly (12 November 1928) *(above left)*, who also typified the Scorpio tendency toward positions of management and power when she became *Princess* Grace of Monaco.

***Above:* Great Britain's Prince Charles (14 November 1948) is exceedingly capable at a vast number of pursuits—in the Fleet Air Arm, he flew jets from aircraft carriers, and is now an apt polo player and a husband to Princess Diana (see Cancer), and heir to the throne. *At right:* Actor Richard Burton (10 November 1925). A powerful actor, he had two tumultuous marriages with Elizabeth Taylor (see Pisces).**

THE SIGNS OF THE ZODIAC
SAGITTARIUS
(The Archer)

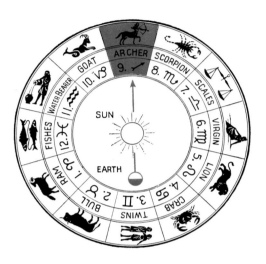

The ninth sign of the zodiac, Sagittarius was known in Hindu astrology as Dhanus. The Sagittarian symbol, as shown above, represents an arrow and a section of bow, typifying aspiration. Sagittarius is usually pictured as a Centaur, half horse and half man, representing the conflict between the philosophical mind and the carnal instinct of conquest. Sagittarius is said to have been named for the Babylonian god of war. (See page 114.)

The Greeks represented this constellation as a centaur in the act of releasing an arrow. They identified him as Crotus, son of Eupheme, the nurse of the Muses. The Romans identified Sagittarius as Chiron, the centaur who accidentally killed himself by dropping one of Hercules' poisoned arrows on his foot.

The Sun is in Sagittarius annually from 23 November to 21 December. Astrologically and astronomically it is the 30-degree arc immediately preceding the Sun's passing over the Tropic of Capricorn, occupying a position along the ecliptic from 240 degrees to 270 degrees. It possesses the mutable quality of the fire element, being positive, hot, dry, changeable, biocorporeal and obeying.

Ruled by Jupiter, king of all planets, Sagittarius in turn rules Hungary, Spain and Saudi Arabia, as well as the Tuscan region of Italy, the Dalmatian Coast of Yugoslavia and such cities as Avignon, Budapest, Cologne, Naples and Sheffield.

The colors by which Sagittarius is characterized range from pale to olive green.

In Sagittarius, the Sun adds brilliance to the magnetism of Jupiter, making this fiery sign powerful and overforceful. The Moon also joins Jupiter to aid individual adaptability and to improve the sign overall—a fine combination to possess if a

At left: Mary, Queen of Scots (7 December 1542) lost her head to impetuous claims on Queen Elizabeth I's throne. *Above:* An in-character Kirk Douglas (9 December 1916) enthusiastically explains the working of a pistol to Joanna Barnes (15 November 1934), a Scorpio. *Above:* Baseball great Joe DiMaggio (25 November 1914) had a short-lived marriage to actress Marilyn Monroe (1 June 1926—see Gemini). A fiery sign, Sagittarians are said to require orderliness and neatness to accomplish all that their great energy allows; Marilyn's habitual impulsiveness was just too much for Joe.

person can stay with his ideals and purposes despite occasional restless spells.

Mercury enlivens Jupiter, producing an active, energetic sign. All good traits are strengthened, except for a tendency to jump to conclusions too quickly. Venus softens the somewhat irritable nature of this sign, but also lessens its energy. Most Sagittarian faults are controllable through Venus. Mars adds activity to Jupiter, which absorbs such influence, generally to excellent advantage, and through it, all Sagittarian traits are reinforced.

In Sagittarius, the double influence of Jupiter gives great strength to the natural qualities of the sign, generally for the best, though any bad traits may also be accentuated. In turn, Saturn curbs the zeal of Jupiter, adding a scholarly touch to the varied energy of this sign.

Being workers, not seekers, Sagittarians often accomplish twice as much as others and will apply themselves to charitable or helpful causes with the same energy that they devote to their own aims. When their time is thus divided, they are often happiest, because by doubling their effort—as they like to do—they can still handle their own affairs along with someone else's. When confronted by adversity or failure, these people can usually stage a remarkable 'comeback' by merely stepping up their activity or their output.

Sagittarians are naturally intuitive, with keen foresight, so when they feel sure that something 'can't go wrong' they yield to impulse. However, in their excitement and enthusiasm, they may overlook new problems that might arise. This impetuosity causes Sagittarians great trouble through middle age, when they become irritable and develop unruly tempers, which can be soothed or restrained only by persons whom they trust. Sometimes they literally wear themselves down until their recklessness is merely spasmodic. With their stamina depleted, they then fuss from one minor project to another, getting nowhere.

At their best and strongest, Sagittarius people insist on seeing things through, and their impulsive actions are contagious, bringing them popularity and many followers. Those who achieve success under this sign are usually neat, methodical and orderly.

In business, Sagittarians succeed in anything that provides a multitude of outlets for their active, versatile minds. They like to travel and do well as prospectors, mining engineers, pilots and sea captains. Imports and exports are good avenues for their progressive, systematic minds. They also do well as bankers and financiers, but in all well-established endeavors they should avoid too many side interests, remembering that time is money.

Inventors, writers and large farm operators are all found under Sagittarius. They are very strong in scientific and mechanical fields, and in a partnership with Aries or Gemini they can achieve great results. The spontaneity of Sagittarius and the exuberance of Leo is also an effective combination, though it may prove less sustained.

Partnerships between Sagittarius and slower-moving signs are generally unproductive. There is one exception: Sagittarius supplies the impulsive fervor that Capricorn needs, making that a good combination. The spontaneity of Sagittarius also combines with the deliberation of Scorpio, but chiefly in big enterprises. In lesser projects they may disagree.

In love and marriage, Sagittarius is aptly called 'the bachelor sign' because these freedom-seeking folk can get along quite well on their own. However, they are cheerful, considerate and willing to share burdens, so potentially they might prove to be fine spouses. Sagittarians do well to marry someone born under their own sign or a person born in Gemini, due to the mutual urge toward varied interests. Sagittarius also may marry well with Aries or Leo, which are themselves impetuous to a degree. Sagittarius and Libra are often a good marital team, due to their mutual recognition of intuitive qualities.

Benjamin Disraeli (21 December 1805) *(above left)* **and William Ewart Gladstone (9 December 1809)** *(above right)*, **were rivals in the nineteenth-century British Parliament. Disraeli was a Conservative, and the latter was a Liberal. However, between the two of them, they dominated British politics, and led the Empire with precision for six Prime Ministerial terms. Entertainer Frank Sinatra (12 December 1915)** *(at right)* **has had several career setbacks that he has overcome with great energy.**

THE SIGNS OF THE ZODIAC
CAPRICORN
(The Goat)

The tenth sign of the zodiac, Capricorn (aka Capricornus) was considered by the ancients to be the most important of all the signs, perhaps because they considered the Winter Solstice to be the point of gravitation that controlled the Sun's orbit. The Capricorn legend may well have begun during the Greek gods' war with the giants, in which they were driven into Egypt and pursued by Typhon. In order to escape, each was forced to change his shape, and Pan, leaping into the Nile, turned the upper part of his body into a goat and lower part into a fish, a shape considered by Jupiter worthy of commemoration as a constellation. (See page 109.) The Capricorn symbol, shown in the chart above, represents the figure by which the sign is often pictured—that of the forepart of a goat, with the tail of a fish— vaguely suggesting the mermaid. Sometimes Capricorn is depicted as a dolphin, or 'sea goat.'

Ptolemy and Tycho Brahe catalogued 28 stars in the area of this constellation, but none of notable size. Literally translated, Capricorn means 'a goat with horns.' Eudoxus mentions Capricorn in the fourth century BC.

The Sun is in Capricorn annually from 22 December to 20 January. Astrologically and astronomically it is the first 30-degrees following the Winter Solstice, marked by the passing of the Sun over the Tropic of Capricorn and occupying a position along the ecliptic from 270 degrees to 300 degrees. It possesses the leading quality of the Earth element, being negative, cold, dry and obeying.

Ruled by Saturn, Capricorn in turn influences such diverse regions on Earth as Bulgaria, India (particularly the Punjab), Lithuania, Mexico and the German states of Hesse and Saxony, as well as the cities of Brussels, Oxford and Port Said.

At far left: Martin Luther King Jr (15 January 1929) was a powerful and magnetic speaker whose belief in God's love for his people led him to orate courageously, even in the most hostile of circumstances. Even in this bright life, there were shadows of despair and falls from grace.

At left: Sir Isaac Newton (25 December 1642), of course, gave us Newton's Law of Gravity and postulated other important views of the physical nature of the universe.

Mohammed Ali (born Cassius Clay on 18 January 1942) stunned the sports world with his lightning-fast fists and 'Float like a butterfly, sting like a bee,' approach to boxing. He became one of the most controversial ring champions of all time. Witty, quick-thinking and unpredictable, Ali also displayed equivocation toward major decisions, such as retirement.

Capricorn's colors, shared in part by Scorpio and Libra, are dark brown and black.

In Capricorn, the Sun modifies the gloom of Saturn, lessening the self-conscious factors of this sign and strengthening its self-reliance. It also guides Capricorn's natural propensity to seek knowledge toward high attainment. On the other hand, the Moon tends to increase moodiness, although the changeability of the Moon can redirect the mind into new channels. The only question is how helpful these changes might be, as the dual influence forces some Capricorns to extremes.

Under this sign, Mercury and Saturn are quite unfavorable, and the intellect of this sign can be diverted to dangerous, unprofitable adventures. Fortunately, Venus combines with Saturn to rouse the Capricorn nature from melancholia to sociability, although this can result in jealousy and misunderstanding.

Mars gives purpose to the moody Saturn, and this combination furthers the development of the Capricorn traits, but can some-times apply to bad as much as good. Jupiter strongly influences Saturn, bringing out the best found in this sign. Due to this influence, people with this combination seem to be typical Capri-cornians, but possessed of more luck and intelligence than most.

In Capricorn, the influence of Saturn is doubled, adding to the practical foresight of this sign. Defeatism, in its turn, is more evident. However, other planetary influences can be used to acti-vate the loftier qualities of this sign. Capricornians have something resembling a psychic sense and are often quite aware of it. Fear of ridicule often curtails their expression of their views, making them secretive, but in a defensive way. They take a dark view of many projects, feeling that they are too difficult, and this in turn causes them to shun the world and seek solitude.

Intellectual Capricornians who fail to broaden their views or accept the more practical side of life are apt to become morose and give themselves over to reckless dissipation. Those who fail to develop their studious qualities at all and who lack the benefit of early cultural training may become utterly despondent and totally unable to combat adverse conditions. Thus, Capricornians need encouragement early in life so they may gain confidence and strengthen their genial and witty qualities. The more gregarious they become, the more diversified and realistic their

interests, the better they can elude the ever-haunting specters of pessimism and despair.

Self-interest is strong in Capricorn, for these people are used to finding their own way. However, those who are fully matured are by no means selfish. Fear of the future often makes them economi-cal, but they share their possessions with others, sometimes too generously. Once a dark mood has passed, a Capricorn person often manages to forget it. Their desire for success is usually so determined that it rouses petty jealousy on the part of others. If Capricornians do not fall victim to despair, they can outlast their problems and overcome all limitations, and thus become true optimists.

In business, people of this sign are good managers, superinten-dents, bookkeepers and accountants. Their pragmatic foresight makes them good financiers. They succeed in many professions, as lecturers, teachers and lawyers, to name a few. They also usually evidence strong literary qualifications. Capricorn and Sagittarius may make exceptional business partners, combining vision with impulse. Capricorn also finds good business associates in Taurus or Virgo. Capricorn and Aquarius do well, proved Aquarius does not hold Capricorn back. The same applies with Capricorn and Cancer, a combination that is pleasant, but apt to fail through Cancer's timidity.

In love and marriage, Capricorn probably does best with Virgo, though Capricorn and Taurus may prove an equally fine union. Capricorn and Aries also promise good marital prospects. All three of those signs have qualities which are helpful to Capricorn's fluctuating moods.

Above: **Both US President Richard Nixon (9 January 1913) and legendary pop star Elvis Presley (8 January 1935) were Capricorns. Both were extraordinarily successful in their respective fields, and both were prone to bouts of despair. Nixon fell into the ferocious—and politically fatal—Watergate Scandal, while Elvis pushed himself into a busy life and a hectic, frenzied concert schedule, which ultimately led to his tragic heart attack on 16 August 1977.**

The legendary Marlene Dietrich (27 December 1901) *(at right)* always had an enigmatic, Capricornish, aspect—as well as a powerful, mysterious personality that seemed to create its very own cinematic atmosphere.

THE SIGNS OF THE ZODIAC
AQUARIUS
(The Water Bearer)

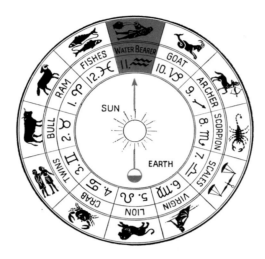

The eleventh sign of the zodiac. The Aquarian symbol, seen in the chart above, represents a stream of water, symbolizing the servant of humanity who pours out the water of knowledge to quench the thirst of the world. Aquarius is thought to represent Ganymede, son of Callirhoe, the most beautiful of mortals, who was carried to heaven by an eagle to act as cup bearer to Jupiter. According to other accounts, however, it is Deucalion, son of Prometheus, who was translated to heaven in memory of the mighty deluge from which only he and Pyrrha were saved.

As a constellation, Aquarius is mentioned by Aratus in the third century BC. Ptolemy catalogued 47 stars in the area; Tycho Brahe, 41. However, there appears to be no record that connects the name Aquarius with any of the stars or configurations within the area. The *Encyclopedia Brittanica* merely states that perhaps the name was chosen because the period when the constellation is tenanted by the Sun is the rainy season. (See page 106.)

The Sun is in Aquarius annually from 21 January to 20 February. Astrologically and astronomically it is the second 30-degree arc following the Sun's passing of the Winter Solstice, occupying a position along the ecliptic from 300 degrees to 330 degrees. It is the fixed quality of the air element, in which the will is largely motivated by reasoning processes, whether sound or unsound. It is positive, hot, moist, sanguine, rational and obeying.

Before the discovery of the planet Uranus in 1781, Aquarius was identified with the planet Saturn. Since the existence of Uranus has become known, astrologers have been inclined to identify it as the ruler of Aquarius. Still others point to Neptune—discovered in 1846—because the persona of its namesake (Neptune, king of the sea) is so starkly similar to that of Aquarius.

Traditionally, Aquarius has been characterized as being the

At left: James Dean (8 February 1931) became a cult figure after his untimely death. A great actor, he suffered when his mother died in 1940, and when his great love, Pier Angeli (19 June 1932), a Gemini, left him unexpectedly. *Above left:* The legendary Humphrey Bogart (23 January 1899) was born in New York City—said to be under the sign of Cancer. He chose Lauren Bacall (see Virgo) as his life's partner. *Above right:* Paul Newman (26 January 1925) is not only a fine actor, but in common with James Dean, has an avid interest in racing cars, and is quite successful on the track.

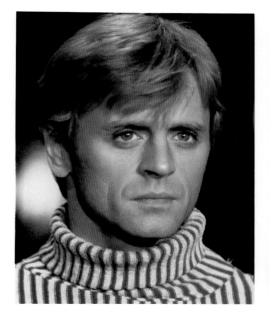

ruling influence over northeastern Europe—Lithuania, Poland, Russia, Sweden and Prussia—as well as such adjacent German city-states as Bremen and Hamburg, which remain *today* as city-states within the borders of the Federal Republic of Germany.

The Aquarian color is, quite simply, sky blue.

In Aquarius, as in other signs, the Sun stimulates Saturn, causing Aquarians to rise from obscurity and develop high-minded purposes and strong characters. Honesty and popularity are furthered by this combination. The Moon, however, may lead the Aquarian to many disappointments. Also, the restless quality of Aquarius is overstressed and must be curbed. However, receptivity aids the trend toward knowledge, and people so influenced can attain great prominence.

In this sign, Mercury and Saturn counterbalance each other somewhat. Quickness and ease of accomplishment to some degree offset the lack of incentive so common to this sign. Honesty and scholarly urges usually control the deceptive ways of Mercury, giving insight to the Aquarian. However, the combination of Venus and Saturn is usually counterproductive, giving this sign a tendency to dissipation, extravagance and reckless ways.

Mars combines well with Saturn, often quite effectively, as purpose is needed in this sign, but Aquarians must guard against the danger of scattering their efforts. Jupiter visibly influences Saturn, giving persons of this sign popularity, and also adds to their ambition. In Aquarius, the double influence of Saturn accentuates intellectual and humanitarian qualities, but can build a double-thick shell as well.

More famous persons have been born under Aquarius than any other sign, and in the great majority of cases they have risen from obscurity or have made up for early failure, sometimes succeeding despite seemingly insurmountable odds. Invariably, they have done this on their own, through the full application of all that they have learned. Self-reliance, confidence and the belief that they are right are the qualities that lay the foundation of their success.

Aquarians who develop the honesty and kindly sentiments of this sign are sure to attain great heights. They have mild dispositions and can curb their tempers. They are both active and volatile, and once their ambitions are sparked, they can scale unprecedented heights. The Aquarian's greatest fault is indolence, for if they delay or treat life lazily, they will never get anywhere. They must also maintain their natural, quiet dignity, for without it, they may become boastful and surly, losing the fame that otherwise may carry them far.

In business, Aquarians are good bargainers, keen buyers, capable auctioneers and make excellent promoters, as they know how to stimulate interest. They do especially well in law and politics. Their mechanical skills are well developed, and many noted scientists, as well as famous inventors, have been born under this sign.

Business partnerships are valuable to Aquarians, who seldom press their opportunities themselves, but require the cooperation of others. They guide Aries people to opportunities and rouse the latent potential of Pisces. Aquarians have a steadying effect on Gemini or Libra, which can work to their mutual advantage.

In love and marriage, Aquarius does well with most signs, for the Aquarian has an understanding nature. Gemini, Leo and Libra are especially good, as they respond strongly to the sympathies of Aquarius.

Above far left: The superb ballet dancer Mikhail Baryshnikov (27 January 1948). *Above middle left:* US President Abraham Lincoln (12 February 1809) was born in a log cabin, but by determination, faith in God and intensive study established the most successful legal practice in the state of Illinois, and went on to become the very great president who kept the Union together during the US Civil War.

Above near left: Frederick the Great of Prussia (24 January 1712). Prussia was a minor kingdom, but the aggressive Frederick swiftly made it one of the mightiest European powers. *At left:* Television personality Victoria Principal (30 January 1945). *Above:* The pervasive confidence of US President Ronald Reagan (6 February 1911) was, for some, a relief from the often tentative tenure of US President Jimmy Carter (see Libra).

THE SIGNS OF THE ZODIAC
PISCES
(The Fishes)

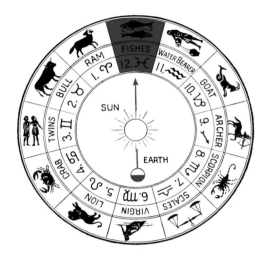

The twelfth and final sign of the traditional zodiac, the Piscean symbol, shown above, represents a pair of great seahorses or sea lions, yoked together, who dwell in the innermost regions of the sea. It is also symbolic of life after death, and of bondage—the inhibiting of self-expression, except through others—as well as of the struggle of the soul within the body. The constellation Pisces is mentioned by Eudoxus in the fourth century BC, and Ptolemy catalogued 38 stars in the area.

In Greek mythology Aphrodite and Eros, surprised by Typhon on the banks of the Euphrates, sought safety in the water and were changed into two fishes. This tale is said to be an adaptation of an earlier Egyptian story. In Roman mythology, the story is the same except that it features Venus and Cupid as the equivalents of Aphrodite and Eros. (See page 113.)

The Sun is in Pisces annually from 21 February to 20 March. Astrologically and astronomically it is the 30-degree arc immediately preceding the passing of the Sun over the point of the Spring Equinox occupying a position along the ecliptic from 330 degrees to 360 degrees. It is the mutable quality of the water element, being negative, cold, moist, obeying and fruitful, as well as effeminate, idle, sickly and unfortunate.

Traditionally thought to have been ruled by Jupiter, Pisces is more properly affiliated with Neptune, a planet that was unknown to all but a select few until 1846. Pisces itself rules *all* of Southeast Asia. Although it would seem strange, the sign of the fish also holds sway over the great Sahara Desert. Indeed, Pisces presides over all of northern Africa, except the old Barbary Coast area and Egypt— but there are some scholars who disagree about Egypt. Also under the Piscean influence are Portugal, Spanish Galicia, France's Nor-

At left: Actor and comedian Jackie Gleason (26 February 1916) exhibited a brilliant sense of comedy. His collaborator Art Carney (4 November 1918), was a Scorpio. *Above left:* US President Andrew Jackson (15 March 1767). Jackson was a soldier, horse fancier and powerful president, expanding the powers of that office greatly during his two terms of office. His strong convictions earned him the name 'Old Hickory.' *Above right:* Country singer Johnny Cash (26 February 1932) has made a career of empathetic songwriting that centers on convicts, affairs of the heart and patriotism.

mandy region and the cities of Alexandria, Cleveland, Ohio and Seville.

The Piscean color is pure, glistening white.

In Pisces, the Sun, combined with Jupiter or Neptune, promises fame and fortune, as well as happiness. The Sun develops all the fine but latent qualities of Pisces, and through its powerful influence, the reliability found in Pisces can lead to great honor. In all, this is one of the finest combinations. The Moon blends naturally with Jupiter. Its lunar influence adds adaptability, but may otherwise be weakening, though with Neptune its effect is often negligible.

Mercury combines well with Jupiter, overcoming the caution of Pisces and finding outlets for the abilities that are usually too latent in this sign. Jupiterian integrity controls the more wayward Mercury, and Venus produces an optimistic outlook, resulting in a happy, cheerful disposition. People with this combination are simple and truthful.

Mars and Jupiter combine almost to perfection, as Pisces needs Martian activity and is *definitely* capable of shaping it. Jupiter has double strength in this sign, but needs other planetary influences to attain high purpose, for without them, the indolence of the sign may prevail. This is perhaps why Neptune has been such a mathematically balancing influence on Pisces.

Saturn provides Pisces with the needed intellectuality to produce a strong philosophy. Pisceans can usually weather disappointments, and if they can shake off morbid moods, this combination can bring them fame as well as popularity.

Because of their unselfish disposition, Pisceans sometimes fail to fully realize their own possibilities. The greater their honesty, the more doubtful they become as to their own ability. This in turn produces fear of the future, which then increases their immediate worries. Subsequently, Pisces people are perhaps the most cautious of all the signs where their own affairs are concerned.

In contrast, however, Pisceans often rely upon the promises of other people and thus are easily and frequently duped. Though they themselves are sincere and trustworthy, they are often

blamed for the mistakes of others, who have shunted the burden onto the kindly Pisces person. Often, a Pisces individual becomes the victim of a subtle, cunning plot, which is never suspected.

There are two saving factors to this sign. One is the optimistic trend inspired by Jupiter. Most other planets would be deadly if they held chief sway over Pisces, but thanks to their jovial dispositions, Pisceans can make their way through deep troubles almost as if they were trifles. The other factor in their behalf is that their true worth is always sincerely appreciated by real friends and good people, who help them to accentuate their strong points and even serve as buffers against unscrupulous persons.

In business, Pisceans tend to gravitate to large organizations, where their honesty and executive capacity can be appreciated. They do well in government jobs and scientific pursuits. Many of them also succeed as engineers. They are interested in historical subjects and all forms of Nature.

Pisces and Aries form a good team in business. Association with Taurus, Virgo and Aquarius also furnishes attractive prospects. Pisces, with its reliability, and Capricorn, with its business acumen, make an excellent partnership in enterprises where each can handle his own area of expertise.

While a marriage between two persons born under Pisces is harmonious, it is difficult for one to bring out the other's more forceful qualities. Pisces would do better in a pairing with Cancer, Virgo or Scorpio, but other signs often prove helpful, with the exception of Libra, which is too prone to weigh the Pisces shortcomings.

Above left: **Distinguished actress Elizabeth Taylor (27 February 1932) won two Academy Awards for her acting, and had two tumultuous marriages with Richard Burton (see Scorpio).** *Above right:* **Guitarist George Harrison (25 February 1943) teamed with John Lennon (see Libra), Paul Mc Cartney (18 June 1942), a Gemini, and Ringo Starr (7 July 1940), a Cancer, to form the phenomenal Beatles, and has since had successes of his own.** *At right:* **The first US President, George Washington (22 February 1732) was of such regal presence that it was first thought to make him *king*, not president.**

THE INFLUENCE OF THE PLANETS

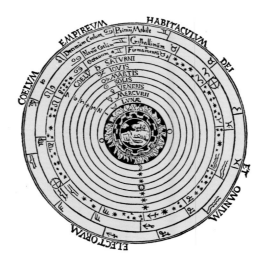

Ancient astrologers linked the planets to different days of the week. In English, the Sun's Day is Sunday, the Moon's Day is Monday. However the names of the Roman gods have become mixed with their Teutonic equivalents. For example, Woden is used instead of Mercury for Woden's Day, or Wednesday, while Thor is used instead of Jupiter for Thor's Day, or Thursday. The French, however, have adhered more closely to the Latin origins, with such names as *mardi*, for Mars' Day, or Tuesday, and *mercredi* for Mercury's Day, or Wednesday, and so on.

Astrologically speaking, each planet is the ruler of its respective day of the week. In astrology, the planetary influences are strongest on the day of a person's birth. Each individual thereby partakes of the planet governing his birth sign, but also comes under the direct influence of the *exact day* on which he was born. This is a factor in its own right, and whether it proves to be a dominating force or simply a modifier of the indications of the birth sign depends to a great degree upon the planets involved and their varied effects upon one another.

From the earliest days of astrology, special note was given to the planets, or 'wanderers,' which followed their own special paths among the fixed stars of constellations that form the signs of the zodiac. These planets—seven in number—were simply the members of the Solar System that were continually visible from Earth, namely: the Sun, the Moon, Mercury, Venus, Mars, Jupiter and Saturn. (According to astronomers and those who believe in a *heliocentric* universe, the Sun and Moon are not technically planets.)

Each sign of the zodiac was regarded as under the control of one special planet. The Sun became the governing influence of Leo, while the Moon held sway over Cancer. The other planets were each given two signs: Mercury controls Gemini and Virgo, with Venus influencing Taurus and Libra, Mars dominating Aries and Scorpio, Jupiter ruling Sagittarius and Pisces, and Saturn governing Capricorn and Aquarius. In recent centuries, however, some astrologers have seen fit to reassign Aquarius to Uranus and Pisces to Neptune. No astrological affiliation is usually attributed to Pluto.

At left: **The Moon as well as the Sun are included by astrologers among the 'planets' that have a dominant influence over each sign.**

Planetary Symbolism:

	Angelic	Formal	Prismatic
The Sun	Michael	Circular	Gold
The Moon	Gabriel	Irregular	Pale, Silvery
Mercury	Raphael	Slender	Gray
Venus	Arnad	Curved	Pale Blue-green
Mars	Samael	Sharp, Angular	Red
Jupiter	Zadkiel	Full, Curved	Deep Royal Purple
Saturn	Cassiel	Short, Straight	Pale Gold
Uranus	Arvath	Broken Lines	Mixed
Neptune	—	Rhythmic Curves	Sea Green to Smoky Blue
Pluto	—	Heavy, Sharp, Angular	Red

THE SUN

The Sun operates chiefly through the anterior pituitary gland, to affect the circulation of the blood through the heart and the arteries, the tear ducts and the spinal cord.

The Sun is the strongest of all planetary influences, so forceful that it can seldom be repressed, though its fine qualities may be neglected or dissipated. Acquisition of knowledge and artistic achievement are keynotes of this influence. The Solarian nature is one that puts ideas into practice, often riding over all obstacles. Often, they are regarded as lucky, but that is because their inherent optimism will not allow them to accept temporary setbacks as failure. Along with such attributes toward success, the Sun denotes a dignity of manner, integrity of nature and loyalty to a cause. It carries the gift of good speaking and a magnetic personality, if effort is made toward their development. The weakness of this nature is found in the neglect of small things, or pressing for personal glory rather than high achievement.

The winged globe in Egyptian art is a familiar representation of the solar orb. Atenism, the first impersonal concept of the Deity, worshipped only 'the power which came from the Sun,' and forbade any emblem or idol that would tend to substitute a symbol for the thing itself. To the Persian it was Mithras; to the Hindu, Brahma; to the Chaldean, Bel; and to the Greek, Adonis and Apollo. In Freemasonry Sol-om-on, the name of the Sun in three languages, is an expression of light.

Below: **The Sun sets on the Golden Gate near San Francisco, California. The Sun is the strongest of planetary influences, and is associated with Leo.**

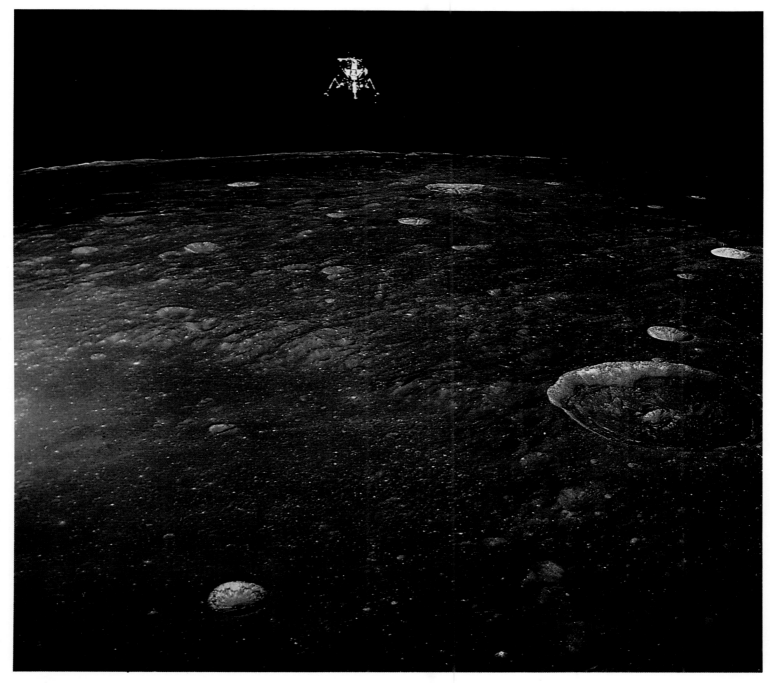

THE MOON

A satellite of the Earth, our Moon has been known to different civilizations as Luna, Soma and Isis (the 'mother of the Earth'). It has given us the name for the first day of the week—Monday—and also to such words and notions as lunacy, lunatic and moonstruck.

The Moon, reflecting the light of the Sun, emits a degree of heat which can be registered by concentrating the rays on the bulb of a thermometer.

The period of the Moon's axial rotation is the same as its period of revolution so that the same side of the Moon is always turned toward the Earth. That its orbit was formerly smaller and its velocity correspondingly greater is proved by comparing records of ancient eclipses to tables based on observation of its present motion.

The Moon is associated with the substance of the body, as distinguished from the vitality flowing through it; the alimentary canal; the child-bearing female organs and functions; the lymphs; the sympathetic nervous system; and the cerebellum (the lower ganglia).

Like the Moon itself, its planetary influence is changeable, yet understandable, and therefore controllable. Imagination is its chief trait and one that can be carried to almost fanciful extremes.

On the one hand, the Lunarian exhibits that insight known as intuition; on the other, overimagination can lead to worry and hysteria. In between, there is a restless, ever-changing trend, which may run the gamut from idle dreaming to compelling urge to become a vagabond or wanderer. Being pliable, the Lunarian nature is receptive and adaptable to almost any circumstance. It betokens sympathy, sound economy and intelligent planning, except when indecision takes hold. Such fluctuation is the great danger of the Lunarian influence.

Above: **The Apollo 12 manned Lunar Module *Intrepid* comes in to land on the Moon's Ocean of Storms in November 1969. The Moon, Cancer's 'planet,' symbolizes irregular forms, pale silvery hues and the Archangel Gabriel.**

MERCURY

A small planet, with pale, bluish light, Mercury is the planet closest to the Sun. Never more than 28 degrees from the Sun, it is rarely visible to the naked eye. The Roman god Mercury and the Greek god Hercules, the winged messenger of the gods, were endowed with the qualities that are associated with the influence of the planet Mercury. To the Chaldeans it was Nego, the planet of warning. It was also associated with Buddha, the wise.

Ancient astrologers theorized the existence of a planet nearer to the Sun than Mercury, to which they gave the name Vulcan, but it has not (as yet) been discovered by astronomers.

Mercury stands for swift action and indicates a convincing speaker. Mercurians think fast, act fast and talk fast. Given a bit of superficial knowledge, they can make it look like intellectual attainment. They are adaptable to almost nay circumstances or conditions. Such are the positive aspects of this planetary influence—positive aspects from the standpoint of the Mercurian himself, since he stands to profit thereby. It is how these natural abilities are applied that marks the good or bad in the Mercurian. When engaged in cooperative, worthwhile efforts, these traits are strongly positive.

Mercury is associated with the thyroid gland; the brain and the cerebro-spinal nervous system; the sense of sight; the tongue and the organs of speech; and with the hands as instruments of intelligence.

At right: **Mercury, as photographed by the Mariner 10 spacecraft on 29 March 1974. Quick-thinking Gemini and Virgo are both 'under' Mercury.**

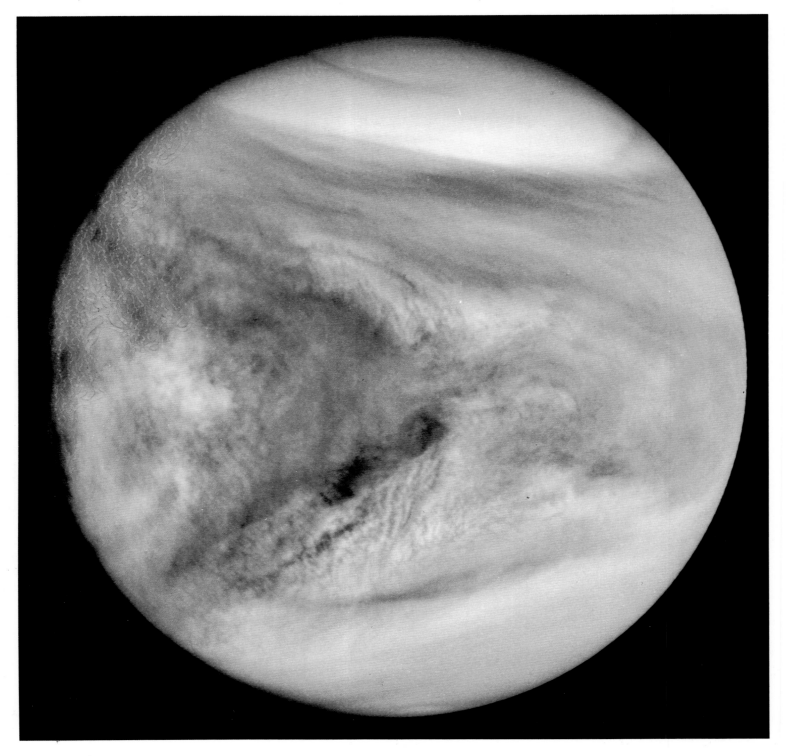

VENUS

A brilliant planet reflecting a silvery-white light, it is the second planet from the Sun, and the most brilliant object that illuminates the evening sky. The Greeks associated it with Aphrodite. To the Romans, it was known as Lucifer, when the 'morning star,' and Vesper, when the 'evening star.' To the Chaldeans it was Ishtar, and compared to the Sumerian virgin mother, the 'Lady of Heaven,' and the goddess of fertility.

Like Mercury, Venus exhibits phases, from a large twin crescent at the inferior conjunction, when it is closest to the Earth, and sometimes visible in daylight if you know where to look for it, to a small, round orb at the superior conjunction, when it is on the opposite side of the Sun from the Earth. After the superior conjunction it is an evening star and thus is visible in the evening sky after sundown, setting later each evening until it reaches it maximum elongation of about 47 degrees—at which time it sets about three hours after the Sun.

Shortly thereafter it attains its greatest brilliancy, then grows rapidly smaller as it again comes closer to the Sun, until at its inferior conjunction it becomes invisible. It then reappears on the other side of the Sun and becomes again visible as the morning star. Its motion as a morning star, as measured from the Earth, is slower because of its greater distance from the Earth: 26 million miles at the inferior conjunction, as compared to 160 million miles at the superior conjunction.

Venus rules the thymus gland; the sense of touch; the throat; kidneys; and to some extent the generative system. Its influence has been said to operate, through the solar plexus, upon the functions of digestion and nutrition. It has an indirect influence upon features, complexion and hair—in so far as those express beauty.

In its highest form, Venus provides the finest of all planetary influences. It denotes a kindly, harmonious nature, with a desire for happiness and comradeship. Beauty, charm, love of music and gaiety, all belong to the Venusian makeup. Persons under this influence will spare no effort in the creation of comfortable surroundings. They enjoy home life and form firm and lasting friendships. Such are the positive aspects.

In contrast, lack of harmony is disturbing to Venusians. They become emotional over disputes. Being kindly, they are easily offended and will resent even slight neglect. Unless they are careful in their choice of friends or those upon whom they shower their affections, misunderstanding may result.

At left: **A Pioneer Orbiter image of Venus. This planet is said to dominate Taurus and Libra, and is both the morning and the evening 'star.'**

MARS

The nearest planet to Earth and frequently visible, Mars may be recognized through its distinct reddish hue. To the Chaldeans it was known as Nergal, the 'raging king' and the 'furious one.' To the Babylonians, it represented the god of war and pestilence, said to preside over the nether-world. For Alchemists, it represented Iron. Mars was known to the Greeks as Ares, the god of war; and as Nimrod, the god of the chase, whose mission it was apparently to dispel terror and fear. To the Greeks, it was Pyrois, the fire. The Romans celebrated the festival of Mars in March, before an altar in the Campus Maritius. From it comes our word martial, warlike—as in martial arts.

In the human body, Mars influences the cortex, or cortical portion, of the adrenal gland; the head, externally; the sense of taste; the breasts and the maternal functions, and in part the generative organs; the motor nerves; the excretory organs; and the red corpuscles of the blood.

Physical drive and energy are basic in the planetary influence of Mars. The Martian nature can be brave to the point of becoming foolhardy, unless tempered by other influences. It gives aggres-siveness to Aries and Scorpio, the signs where it predominates.

Fortunately, the Martian influence can be diverted. With it, attainment of an immediate goal is so important that other purposes can be shelved. Here is a fighting instinct that knocks down all obstacles, small and large. Keep them small when they do not matter, large, when they are important, and you have the ultimate in Martian development.

Sports, adventure and love of outdoor life all are found in the martian personality. Travel, military affairs and any form of new and virile experience appeals to those who come under this influence. Skill and mechanical ability are part of the Martian setup; and as natural concomitants, honesty and reliability go into such a nature. Such are the positive aspects. In contrast, the Martian influence can breed impatience, savagery, boastfulness and a tendency toward useless, wasteful combat.

Action is just another word for Mars, in the full sense of the term. In order to obtain it, persons swayed by this influence may become destructive. When they are prone to envy, nothing can stop their rash, impetuous nature, except their own power of reason, which fortunately is strong and therefore helpful.

Below: **Mars' aggressive red hue is even more pronounced in this 11 July 1976 Viking Orbiter closeup. Aries and Scorpio are its subjective signs.**

JUPITER

The largest planet in the solar system, Jupiter is exceeded in brightness by Venus only because of her greater proximity to the Earth. To the Greeks, is was known as Zeus. It was also associated with Marduk, one of the gods of the Pantheon, and was known to the Hindus as Brahmanaspati.

Jupiter rules the posterior pituitary gland; the feet; the thighs, the liver; the intestines; blood plasma; the muscles; and growth. It also controls the shoulders and arms in motions that for effectiveness depend upon good timing.

In contrast to the highly negative Mars, Jupiter is perhaps the finest and most beneficial of all planetary influences. Though it lacks the inspiration of the Sun, it more than makes up for it in a practical way. People swayed by this influence are friendly, generous and appreciative of others, and therefore cooperative. Sincerity and sympathy go into the Jupiterian nature. Hence, they are honest, charitable and impelled by high ideals. They have open minds and are always ready to take up a worthwhile cause. This automatically makes them popular, and their very frankness often makes them wonder why they are so well liked. Such are the positive aspects of Jupiter.

It would seem that a nature so influenced would be free from all faults, but such is not the case. With a Jupiterian, natural generosity leads to extravagance. Since Jupiterians like people, they in turn like to be liked. Hence, they are easily influenced and will waste their ability as well as their resources in futile, worthless effort. They become careless both of themselves and of their future.

Wastefulness is, therefore, the negative aspect of the Jupiterian nature. Recognition of this can lead to simple, yet vital, ways of correcting the fault; but often, other planetary influences are needed to insure such a result. By all means, Jupiterians must avoid the pitfalls of less fortunate influences, for in itself Jupiter is highly favorable.

Above: **The largest, 'kindliest' planet is Jupiter (seen here in a Voyager spacecraft photo) under whose influential sway are Sagittarius and Pisces.**

SATURN

The planet next smaller in magnitude to Jupiter, and next more remote from the Sun, Saturn is remarkable for its engirdling system of rings. It was the most remote planet known to the ancients. The surface of Saturn shows markings somewhat similar to those of Jupiter, but fainter. Observations by the Voyager spacecraft have confirmed the theory that the astrologers' ancient theory that the rings are composed of a dense swarm of small, solid particles. Of the satellites of Saturn, the brightest is Titan. When the alchemists and early chemists used the name Saturn, they referred to its association with the metal lead. Lead poisoning was once called the Saturnine colic.

Saturn was the ancient Roman god of the seed sowing. His temple in Rome, founded in 497 BC, was used as a state treasury. In 217 BC, the worship of Saturn was conformed to that of its Greek counterpart, Cronus, son of Uranus, and god of boundless time and the cycles. There was a myth that Saturn in Italy, as with Cronus in Greece, had been king during an ancient golden age—and hence was the founder of Italian civilization.

Saturn is also associated with the Greek god Phoenon, 'the cruel one,' and the Assyrian god Ninib, patron of agriculture, and one of the gods of the pantheon. From it we have the English word saturnian, or saturnine.

Saturn influences the medullary portion of the adrenal gland; the skin and the secretive system; teeth; bones, joints and tendons—particularly the knee and the calf of the leg; the spleen; and sense of hearing.

With the urge for knowledge, the Saturnian nature cultivates other desirable qualities. Such people are patient, serious and reserved in manner. They often remain calm under stress, depending upon their training and intelligence to carry them through. They are sticklers for punctuality and accuracy, and they are usually quite thrifty. These are the positive aspects, but they are innate, rather than acquired.

Constant study can cause Saturnians to draw themselves apart from the world. Patience can lead to procrastination. Seriousness can make them skeptical. Their reserve may become a form of mistrust. Their thrifty ways may turn stingy, and they may therefore resort to deceit to protect their interests. All this can add up to the moodiest of natures. Far from being baleful, however, Saturnian influence is scholarly and scientific.

Among the recently discovered planets, Uranus and Neptune have been given Aquarius and Pisces as respective, tentative zodiacal affiliations. In anatomical terms, Uranus is associated with the parathyroid gland; the brain and nervous system; and the electric and magnetic emanations. Neptune is said to rule the pineal gland and the organs of extrasensory perception, as well as intuitive and psychic receptivity, while Pluto presides over the pancreas and the digestive glands and enzymes, which effect catalytic and hydrolytic transformations essential to proper metabolism.

Below: **Saturn as photographed by Voyager 2 on 4 August 1981. This planet, girdled by its rings, is symbolically a patron of meditative restraint, but negatively connotes brooding. It dominates Capricorn and Aquarius.**

The Influence of the Planets:

Having determined the ruling planet of a person's birthday, its influences can be studied according to general planetary indications (as already listed), as these apply in all combinations of planets. However, the planet of the day is a strongly individual factor, so it is possible to list its influence on the various signs.

The Sun has a strengthening and often beneficent influence on the planets governing each sign, often promising high achievement in fields to which the individual is most suited, but at the same time producing a great intensity which may lead to overeffort. The Moon has a weakening effect on other planets and is therefore generally unfavorable when it predominates, unless the individual can rise above it, which is often possible when his horoscope shows minor planetary influences of a strengthening sort.

Invariably, Venus supplies sympathy to any nature and often in a helpful way, but this planetary influence must be controlled or it can disintegrate into maudlin sentiment and its attendant faults. Jupiter, as a favorable planet, combines well with the others, except in a few instances that will be noted under their respective signs. Though Saturn is generally regarded as unfavorable, its intellectual qualities can prove a valuable influence in most planetary combinations. Faults are usually intensified by Saturn. Hence, other planetary influences must be stressed to counteract them.

To determine this modifier, one should use the following tables adapted from Walter and Litzka Gibson's *Book of the Psychic Sciences*:

Year 1900 — Value I
Other years in 1900s and their values:

01	02	03	*04*	05	06	07	*08*	09	10	11	*12*	13	14	15	*16*	17	18	19	*20*
29	30	31	*32*	33	34	35	*36*	37	38	39	*40*	41	42	43	*44*	45	46	47	*48*
57	58	59	*60*	61	62	63	*64*	65	66	67	*68*	69	70	71	72	73	74	75	76
85	86	87	*88*	89	90	91	*92*	93	94	95	*96*	97	98	99					
2	3	4	5	0	1	2	3	5	6	0	1	3	4	5	6	1	2	3	4
						21	22	23	*24*	25	26	27	*28*						
						49	50	51	*52*	53	54	55	*56*						
						77	78	79	*80*	81	82	83	*84*						
						6	0	1	2	4	5	6	0						

Years in italics (*04, 08,* etc) are *leap years* and 1 point must be added to their values for any date from 1 March on through the year. Thus, for a date in January or February 1972, the year's value would be 6; for a date in any other month, 7.

Regular Monthly Values

January	0	April	6	July	6	October	0
February	3	May	1	August	2	November	3
March	3	June	4	September	5	December	5

Daily Values
Add from 1 to 31, inclusive, according to exact date.

Ruling Planet as Represented by Total Values

Sun	Moon	Mars	Mercury	Jupiter	Venus	Saturn
1	2	3	4	5	6	7
8	9	10	11	12	13	14
15	16	17	18	19	20	21
22	23	24	25	26	27	28
29	30	31	32	33	34	35
36	37	38	39	40	41	42
43	44	45	46	47	48	49

For dates in the 1800s, add 2 toward total value.
For dates in the 1700s, add 4 toward the total value.

The following examples will clarify the process:

5 April 1957: Year ('57) = 2. Month (April) = 6. Day (5th) = 5. Total values: 2 + 6 + 5 = 13. Ruling planet: Venus.

13 May 1964: Year ('64) = 3 + 1 (leap year). Month (May) = 1. Day (13th) = 13. Total values: 4 + 1 + 13 = 18. Ruling planet: Mercury.

12 September 1897: Year ('97) = 3. Month (September) = 5. Day (12th) = 12. Added value for date in 1800s = 2. Total values: 3 + 5 + 12 + 2 = 22. Ruling planet: the Sun.

To find the ruling planet of George Washington's birthday: 22 February 1732. Year ('32) = 5 + 0 (Leap year but before March 1.) Month (February) = 3. Day (22nd) = 22. Add value for date in 1700s = 4. Total values: 5 + 3 + 22 + 4 = 34. Ruling planet: Venus.

Note: Washington's birthday—and others prior to 1752—were originally figured according to the obsolete Julian calendar. The correct date (22 February 1732) conforms to the Gregorian calendar, which should be used in all astrological calculations.

THE CONSTELLATIONS

T he 48 original, traditional constellation figures have been a source of annoyance to modern astronomers, who have naturally failed to trace among the stars the slightest resemblance to the objects they are supposed to represent. To those actively engaged in a study of stellar and constellation influences, however, these seemingly fanciful shapes are, in reality, a fair representation of the collective influences of the stars contained in them.

Canis Major—the constellation of the Dog—for example, actually influences dogs. This, of course, may be explained by assuming that the ancients based the figures and divisions upon their knowledge of the influence of each.

The difficulty confronting the student of astrology is that each constellation occupies a fairly large part of the heavens and overlaps others when referred to the zodiac. It seems, however, that the major points of influence lie in the vicinity of the important stars and also near the boundary of the influence, which thus appears to play the same part as the cusp of a house.

It must be remembered that a star may have its own effect apart from that of the constellation, which is the group influence of many stars, and therefore, the two must be separated when endeavoring to fix the most sensitive points. It is also extremely

At left: **Clearly seen in this photograph are the three diagonal 'belt' stars and the dangling sword of the constellation Orion, the hunter.**

likely that there may be sub-influences in each constellation, perhaps varying with the part of the figure on which a given group of stars may lie, and this is a matter that will certainly require attention in the future. In practice, it will be found that the effect of the constellation is most marked when the Sun, Moon or Ascendant is posted there. The conjunction, opposition and parallax have effect, but the influence of aspects cannot be traced.

Ptolemy expressed the nature of the constellations in terms of the planets and Sepharial suggested that the signs themselves might not be the real originators of all the influences ascribed to them, some of which might more properly be attributed to constellations. Thus, in the case of Cancer, the pushing nature of its natives may really be due to Monoceros, their love of dogs to Canis Major, and their love of the sea to Argo.

This should be borne in mind, for by careful research we may eventually be able to assign more exact influences to both signs and stars. In this connection it will be obvious that the separate influence of each degree of the zodiac may also be a stellar phenomenon.

In the descriptions that follow, the legendary history of the constellations has been given so that students of symbology and occultism may exercise their powers of interpretation. In all cases, however, the Biblical parallels have been omitted, partly because they are often obvious, but chiefly because they are later importations and not so worthy of study.

The 48 Cardinal constellations known to the ancients.

Zodiacal Constellations

Aries	Gemini	Sagittarius
Aquarius	Leo	Scorpio
Cancer	Libra	Taurus
Capricorn	Pisces	Virgo

Northern Constellations

Andromeda	Cygnus	Pegasus
Aquila	Delphinus	Perseus
Auriga	Draco	Sagitta
Bootes	Equuleus	Serpens
Cassiopeia	Hercules	Triangulum
Cepheus	Lyra	Ursa Major
Corona Borealis	Ophiuchus*	Ursa Minor

Southern Constellations

Ara	Cetus*	Hydra
Argo	Corona Australis	Lepus
Canis Major	Corvus	Lupus
Canis Minor	Crater	Orion
Centaurus	Eridanus	Piscis Australis

* Considered by some to be a zodiacal constellation.

Andromeda: The Chained Woman (20N—55N)

Andromeda was the daughter of Cepheus, the King of Ethiopia, and Cassiopeia. In consequence of Cassiopeia's boast that the beauty of Andromeda surpassed that of the Nereids, Neptune sent a sea monster (Cetus) to lay waste to the country, and promised deliverance only on condition that Andromeda were offered as a sacrifice to it. She was accordingly chained to a rock, but was discovered and released by Perseus, who, riding through the air on Pegasus, slew the monster by turning it to stone with Medusa's Head, and then claimed Andromeda as his bride.

According to Ptolemy, the influence of this constellation is similar to that of Venus, though the legend would lead one to suppose some connection with Virgo. It is said to bestow purity of thought, virtue, honor and dignity upon its natives, but to cause battle with chimerical fears and a tendency to become easily discouraged. Andromeda is associated by the Kabalists with the Hebrew letter Pe and the seventeenth Tarot trump, 'The Stars.' If Mars afflicts the luminaries from Andromeda, and especially if in an angle, it causes death by hanging, decapitation, crucifixion or impalement.

Aquarius: The Water Carrier (5N—30S)

Aquarius is said to represent Ganymede, son of Callirhoe, the most beautiful of mortals, who was carried to heaven by an eagle

Below: **A deep space photograph of the Great Galaxy in the constellation Andromeda, whose influence is said to be like that of the sign Virgo.**

to act as cup bearer to Jupiter. According to other accounts, however, it is Deucalion, son of Prometheus, who was translated to heaven in memory of the mighty deluge from which only he and Pyrrha were saved.

Ptolemy observes that, 'The stars in the shoulders of Aquarius operate like Saturn and Mercury; those in the left hand and in the face do the same; those in the thighs have an influence more consonant with that of Mercury, and in a less degree with that of Saturn; those in the stream of water have power similar to that of Saturn, and moderately to that of Jupiter.' (See page 86.)

To the Kabalists, Aquarius is associated with the Hebrew letter Nun and the fourteenth Tarot trump, 'Temperance,' over which virtue the constellation appears to have some rule. The beauty of Ganymede and his flight through the air also link it to the ideas of personal charm and aviation, with which it is certainly connected.

Aquila: The Eagle (22N—13S)

Originally called Vultur Volans or the Flying Grype, Aquila represents the Eagle, thought to be Jupiter himself, that carried Ganymede to heaven. (See Aquarius)

According to Ptolemy, the influence of Aquila is similar to that of Mars and Jupiter. It is said to give great imagination, strong passions, indomitable will, a dominating character, influence over others, clairvoyance, a keen, penetrating mind and ability for

Below: **A telescopic closeup of the Nebula in Aquila, the eagle. Its qualities are those of great imagination, indomitable will and dominance.**

chemical research. It has always been associated with the sign Scorpio, and by the Kabalists with the Hebrew letter Vav and the sixth Tarot trump, 'The Lovers.'

Ara: The Altar (47S—65S)

During the war between the gods and titans, the gods leagued themselves together and swore to withstand their enemies, confirming their oath upon an altar built for them by the Cyclops. After their victory the altar was taken up to heaven to commemorate the good resulting from unity. According to another account, Ara was the altar on which the Centaur offered his sacrifices.

According to Ptolemy, its influence is similar to that of Venus and also Mercury in some degree. It is said to give aptness in science, egoism, devotion and a love of ecclesiastical matters.

Argo Navis: The Ship Argo (15S—65S)

This constellation represents the ship in which Jason brought the Golden Fleece from Cochis, said to be the first ship ever built.

According to Ptolemy, the bright stars are like Saturn and Jupiter. Argo is said to give prosperity in trade and voyages, and strength of mind and spirit, but it has been observed to accompany cases of drowning. A notable instance of this is furnished by the horoscope of Shelley, where Argo occupied the 8th house and contained the Sun, Venus and Uranus. Drowning is particularly to be feared when Saturn afflicts the Moon in, or from, Argo. It is probably on account of this constellation that Virgo, especially the first decanate, is frequently found to be connected with drowning.

Aries: The Ram (0N—27N)

Aries represents the ram with the Golden Fleece, a gift from Mercury, upon which Phrixus and his sister Helle escaped through the air from their stepmother Ino. Upon arriving in Cochis, Phrixus sacrificed the ram to Jupiter and its fleece was hung in the Grove of Mars, whence it was subsequently carried away by Jason. According to another account it was the ram that guided Bacchus to a spring of water in the Libyan desert. (See page 46.)

Ptolemy observes that, 'The stars in the head of Aries possess an influence similar in their effect to that of Mars and Saturn; those in the mouth act similarly to Mercury, and in some degree to Saturn; those in the hinder foot, to Mars; those in the tail, to Venus.' Aries is associated by the Kabalists with the Hebrew letter Hé and the fifth Tarot trump, 'The Pope.'

Auriga: The Charioteer (30N—60N)

Auriga represents Erichthonius, the son of Vulcan and the King of Athens, who was the first to devise a chariot, drawn by four horses, which he used in order to conceal his greatly deformed feet. The goat and kids depicted in the constellation figure commemorate the goat upon whose milk Jupiter was reared, together with her offspring.

According to Ptolemy, the bright stars are like Mars and Mercury. The constellation is said to give self-confidence, interest in social and educational problems and happiness, but danger of great vicissitudes. The native is fond of country life and may be a teacher or have responsibility for the upbringing of young people. By the Kabalists, Auriga is associated with the Hebrew letter Samech and the 15th Tarot trump, 'The Devil.'

Bootes: The Herdsman (10N—55N)

Bootes is said to be Arcas, whose mother Callisto was transformed into a bear (See Ursa Major) by Juno. While hunting, Arcas came upon his mother in the form of a bear and, unaware it was she, pursued her into the temple of Jupiter, where he would have killed her and afterwards been killed himself by the priests. In order to prevent this, Jupiter, who had taken pity on them, took them both into heaven, where Bootes is still seen pursuing the bear. According to another account, Bootes is Icarius, who was killed by some shepherds he had made drunk with a flagon of wine given him by Bacchus. In consideration of the grief of his daughter Erigone and their hound Maera, Jupiter placed her father in heaven as Bootes, together with herself as Virgo and the hound as Canis Minor.

According to Ptolemy, the influence of the constellation is like that of Mercury and Saturn, though the star Arcturus is like Mars and Jupiter. It is said to give prosperity from work, strong desires, a tendency to excess and fondness for rural pursuits, together with some liking for occultism. The Kabalists associate it with the Hebrew letter Teth and the ninth Tarot trump, 'The Hermit.'

Cancer: The Crab (2N—40N)

This constellation represents the crab that bit the heel of Hercules during his fight with the Lernean Hydra, and it was placed amongst the stars in gratitude by Juno, the enemy of Hercules. (See page 58.)

Ptolemy observes that, 'The two stars in the eyes of Cancer are of the same influence as Mercury, and are also moderately like Mars. Those in the claws are like Saturn and Mercury.' By the Kabalists, Cancer is associated with the Hebrew letter Tzaddi and the eighteenth Tarot trump, 'The Moon.'

Canis Major: The Greater Dog

This constellation is said to represent the dog sent by Jupiter to guard Europa, whom he had stolen and conveyed to Crete. According to other accounts, however, it was either Laelaps, the hound of Actaeon; that of Diana's nymph Procris; that given by Aurora to Cephalus; or finally, one of the dogs of Orion.

Ptolemy states that the stars of this constellation, with the exception of Sirius, are like Venus. It is said to give good qualities, charity and a faithful heart, but violent and dangerous passions. There is some danger from, or fear of, darkness and the night, and liability to dog bites, though the latter characteristic is probably to be associated more particularly with Sirius. Canis Major is connected by the Kabalists with the Hebrew letter Tzaddi and the eighteenth Tarot trump, 'The Moon.'

Canis Minor: The Lesser Dog (1N—10N)

Canis Minor represent Maera, the hound of Icarius, who drowned himself out of his grief at the death of his master. (See Bootes). According to another account, it was Helen's dog who was lost in the Euripus.

Ptolemy gives no information as to the influence of the constellation itself, but merely describes that of its chief star, Procyon. By other authors, however, it is said to cause frivolity and either love of dogs or danger of dog bites. It is noteworthy that the ideas of water and drowning seem to be universally associated with this constellation, for in addition to the Greek ideas embodied in the legends, its Euphratean name was the Water-Dog and its Chinese equivalent Nan Ho, the Southern River, certain of the stars being

called Shwuy Wei, a Place of Water. Together with Canis Major, this constellation is associated by the Kabalists with the Hebrew letter Tzaddi and the eighteenth Tarot trump, 'The Moon.'

Capricorn: The Goat (10S—35S)

During their war with the giants, the gods were driven into Egypt and pursued by Typhon. In order to escape, each was forced to change his shape, and Pan, leaping into the Nile, turned the upper part of his body into a goat and the lower part into a fish, a shape considered by Jupiter worthy of commemoration in the heavens. (See page 82.)

Ptolemy observes that, 'The stars in the horns of Capricorn have efficacy similar to that of Venus, and partly to that of Mars. The stars in the mouth are like Saturn, and partly like Venus; those in the feet and in the belly act in the same manner as Mars and Mercury; those in the tail are like Saturn and Jupiter.' This constellation is associated by the Kabalists with the Hebrew letter Yod and the tenth Tarot trump, 'The Wheel of Fortune.'

Cassiopeia: The Seated Woman (50N—70N)

Cassiopeia, the wife of Cepheus and mother of Andromeda, was taken into heaven in consideration of the deeds of Perseus. (See Andromeda.) She is said to have boasted that not only Andromeda,

Below: A US Naval Observatory photo of a nebula in Cassiopeia, the seated woman. This is a haughty, sometimes overweening influence.

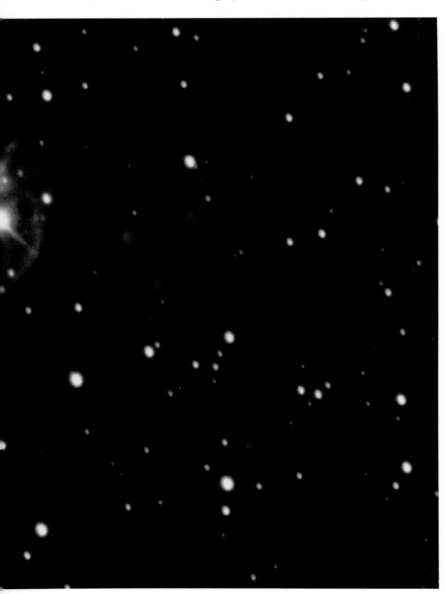

but she herself as well, was fairer than the Nereids, and for that reason she was bound to her chair and condemned to circle the pole with her head downwards as a lesson in humility.

According to Ptolemy, this constellation is of the nature of Saturn and Venus. Cassiopeia is said to give haughtiness, boastfulness and exaggerated pride, but at the same time the power of commanding respect. It is associated by the Kabalists with the Hebrew letter Beth and the second Tarot trump, 'The High Priestess.'

Centaurus: The Centaur (28S—68S)

This constellation probably represents Pholos, son of Silenus and Melia, who was accidentally wounded in the foot by one of Hercules' poisoned arrows. According to some accounts it is Chiron, but he is more correctly associated with Sagittarius.

According to Ptolemy, the stars in the human part of the figure are of the nature of Venus and Mercury, and the bright stars in the horse's part of Venus and Jupiter. It is said to give hard-heartedness, inclination to vengeance, love of arms, strong passions and an energetic nature. Centaurus may also be connected with poison.

Cepheus (55N—85N)

Cepheus, the King of Ethiopia, was taken into heaven with his wife Cassiopeia and his daughter Andromeda in commemoration of the deeds of Perseus. (See Andromeda.)

According to Ptolemy, Cepheus is like Saturn and Jupiter. It gives authority and a sober mind, sometimes making its natives judges or arbitrators, but it also exposes them to cruel and severe trials. If Mars afflicts the luminaries from Cepheus, especially if in an angle, it causes death by hanging, decapitation, crucifixion or impalement. By the Kabalists, this constellation is associated with the Hebrew letter Shin and the twenty-second Tarot trump, 'The Fool.'

Cetus: The Whale or Sea Monster (10N—30S)

Cetus represents the sea monster sent by Neptune to devour Andromeda. (See Andromeda.) For those who believe in a 14-sign zodiac, Cetus is one of the zodiacal constellations.

According to Ptolemy, this constellation is like Saturn. It is said to cause laziness and idleness, but to confer an emotional and charitable nature, with ability to command.

Corona Australis: The Southern Crown (36S—45S)

This is said by some authors to represent a cast-off garland once worn by Sagittarius, while others consider that it represents the wheel upon which Ixion was tormented because of his insult to Juno. This constellation has also been called Uraniscus because of its resemblance to the palate, or roof, of the mouth.

According to Ptolemy, the bright stars are like Saturn and Jupiter. The Corona Australis is said to bring unforeseen troubles, but to also give a position of authority.

Corona Borealis: The Northern Crown (27N—33N)

Corona Borealis represents the garland given by Venus to Ariadne on the occasion of her marriage to Bacchus after she had been forsaken by Theseus.

According to Ptolemy, it is like Venus and Mercury, in that it is said to give artistic ability, love of flowers, lassitude and disillusionment, yet to bring its natives to a position of command. This constellation is associated by the Kabalists with the Hebrew letter Daleth and the fourth Tarot trump, 'The Emperor.'

Corvus: The Crow (7S—25S)

Apollo gave a feast to Jupiter and, requiring water, sent the crow with a cup (Crater) to fetch some. On his way the crow noticed a fig tree and, resting there until the figs became ripe, feasted himself upon them. Then, remembering his errand and fearing the anger of Apollo, he picked up a snake (Hydra), and on his return gave as an excuse that it had prevented him from filling the cup. As punishment, Apollo ordained that the crow should never drink so long as figs were not ripe, and placed the crow, cup and snake in the heavens as a memorial.

According to Ptolemy, Corvus is like Mars and Saturn. It is said to give craftiness, greediness, ingenuity, patience, revengefulness, passion, selfishness, lying, aggressiveness and material instincts, and sometimes causes its natives to become agitators.

Crater: The Cup (5S—23S)

This constellation represents the cup given by Apollo to the crow. (See Corvus.)

According to Ptolemy, it is like Venus and, in some degree, like Mercury. It gives a kind, generous, cheerful, receptive, passionate and hospitable nature, with good mental abilities, but subject to apprehension and indecision. There is a disordered life full of sudden and unexpected events, and great danger of unhappiness, but usually some eminence.

Cygnus: The Swan (28N—55N)

In order to visit Leda, the wife of Tyndareus, the King of Sparta, with whom he was in love, Jupiter turned himself into a swan and, when pursued by Venus in the shape of an eagle, flew to Leda as if for protection.

Cygnus gives a contemplative, dreamy, cultured and adaptable nature. The affections are ill-regulated and unsteady, and the talents develop late. There is some love of water, swimming and the arts. It is associated by the Kabalists with the Hebrew letter Résh and the twentieth Tarot trump, 'Judgment.'

Delphinus: The Dolphin (3N—19N)

When Amphitrite, who was sought as a wife by Neptune, hid herself, the god sent messengers to find her. The dolphin was the first to succeed and was able to persuade her to consent to the marriage. For this service, Neptune placed him in the heavens. According to other accounts it is one of the pirates who were changed into dolphins by Bacchus on his voyage to Ariadne.

According to Ptolemy, Delphinus is like Saturn and Mars. It gives a simple appearance, cheerfulness, dissembling and duplicity and a love of hunting and sport in general, but little happiness. There is a fondness for pleasure, ecclesiastical matters and travel, but also danger of suffering from ingratitude.

Draco: The Dragon (63N—81N)

Draco represents the dragon that guarded the golden apples in the garden of the Hesperides. According to other accounts, however, it is either the dragon thrown by the giants at Minerva in their war with the gods, or the serpent Python slain by Apollo after the deluge.

According to Ptolemy, the bright stars are like Saturn and Mars. Draco gives an artistic and emotional, but somber nature, a penetrating and analytical mind, much travel and many friends, but danger of robbery and of accidental poisoning. It was said by the ancients that when a comet was here, poison was scattered over the world. Draco is associated by the Kabalists with the Hebrew letter Mem and the thirteenth Tarot trump, 'Death.'

Equuleus: The Foal (0N—12N)

According to various accounts, Equuleus represents Celeris, the brother of Pegasus, or Cylarus, the horse of Pollux. It gives friendship and sagacity, but also frivolity and love of pleasure.

This constellation is not to be confused with Equuleus Pictoris (The Painter's Easel), located at 45S—65S, which was identified by La Caille in 1752 and which is usually known by the name Pictor.

Eridanus: The River (0S—55S)

Eridanus represents the River Padus, or Po, into which Phaeton fell when slain by Jupiter in punishment for setting the world on fire when he misguided the chariot of his father Phoebus.

According to Ptolemy, all the stars—with the exception of Achernar—are like Saturn. Eridanus gives a love of knowledge and science, much travel and many changes and a position of authority, but also danger of accidents, especially at sea, and of drowning.

Gemini: The Twins (13N—35N)

This constellation represents Castor and Pollux, the twin sons of Leda and Jupiter, although it has also been suggested that it may represent Apollo and Hercules. (See page 54.)

Ptolemy observes that, 'The stars in the feet of Gemini have an influence similar to that of Mercury, and moderately to that of Venus. The bright stars in the thighs are like Saturn.' It is said to cause trouble and disgrace, sickness, loss of fortune, affliction and danger to the knees. Gemini is associated by the Kabalists with the Hebrew letter Qoph and the nineteenth Tarot trump, 'The Sun.'

Hercules: The Kneeling Giant (5N—53N)

This constellation was put into the heavens as a reminder of the labors of Hercules. According to another account, however, during the war between the gods and titans, the former all ran to one side of the heavens, which would have fallen had not Atlas and Hercules supported it, and the latter was placed in the sky in commemoration of this service.

According to Ptolemy, it is like Mercury. It is said to give strength of character, tenacity and fixity of purpose, an ardent nature and dangerous passions. By the Kabalists it is associated with the Hebrew letter Daleth and the fourth Tarot trump, 'The Emperor.'

Hydra: The Water Snake (10N—36S)

This constellation represents the snake picked up and taken to Apollo by the crow. (See Corvus.)

According to Ptolemy, the bright stars are like Saturn and Venus. It is said to give an emotional and passionate nature, though threatened by great troubles, and to cause some interest in shipping.

Leo: The Lion (0N—34N)

This constellation represents the Nemean Lion, originally from the Moon, that was slain by Hercules.

Ptolemy observes that, 'Of the stars in Leo, two in the head are like Saturn and partly like Mars. The three in the neck are like Saturn, and in some degree like Mercury... Those in the loins... Saturn and Venus; those in the thighs resemble Venus and, in some degree, Mercury.' (See page 62.)

It is said that the stars in the neck, back and wing all bring trouble, disgrace and sickness affecting the part of the body ruled by the sign, especially if they happen to be in conjunction with the Moon. Leo is associated by the Kabalists with the Hebrew letter Kaph and the eleventh Tarot trump, 'Strength.'

Leo is not be confused with Leo Minor (The Lesser Lion), located at 27N—45N, which was identified by Hevelius in 1690, although Leo Minor does give a generous, noble and peaceable,

The contemplative, dreamy, cultured and adaptable nature of the influence of Cygnus, the swan, gives rise to metaphysical speculation concerning its distinction as the celestial home of the North American Nebula (at right).

but fearless nature, with the ability to undertake prominent and responsible positions.

Lepus: The Hare (14S—25S)

A young man of the Isle of Leros greatly desired a hare and brought some over, for none were to be found on the island. The other inhabitants also wished to keep hares, but eventually the animals multiplied to such an extent that there was not enough food for them and they devoured the corn in the fields, whereupon the inhabitants joined together and destroyed them all.

According to Ptolemy, Lepus is like Saturn and Mercury. It gives a quick wit, timidity, circumspection, fecundity and defiance.

Libra: The Balance, or Scales (7S—24S)

Libra was not actually considered a separate constellation by the ancients and was called Chelae, or the Claws of Scorpio, which sign was made to consist of 60 degrees. The present constellation figure is said to represent the balance where in Astraea weighed the deeds of men and presented them to Jupiter. (See page 70.)

Ptolemy observes that, 'Those stars at the points of the claws of Scorpio operate like Jupiter and Mercury; those in the middle of the claws, like Saturn, and in some degree like Mars.' The Kabalists associate Libra with the Hebrew letter Heth and the eighth Tarot trump, 'Justice.'

Lupus: The Wolf (34S—57S)

The wolf is said to be placed in the heavens as a reminder of the religious nature of Chiron the Centaur, who is depicted as spearing it in order to offer it as a sacrifice.

According to Ptolemy, the bright stars are like Saturn and partly like Mars. Lupus is said to give an acquisitive, grasping, aggressive, prudent and treacherous nature, with a keen desire for knowledge and strong, ill-regulated passions.

Lyra: The Lyre (28N—47N)

Mercury found the body of a tortoise cast up from the Nile, and discovered that by striking the sinews after the flesh was consumed a musical note was obtained. He made a lyre of similar shape, having three strings, and gave it to Orpheus, the son of Calliope, who by its music enchanted the beasts, birds and rocks. After Orpheus was slain by the Thracian women, Jupiter placed the lyre in heaven at the request of Apollo and the Muses. This constellation was often called Vultur Cadens, or the Falling Grype, by the ancients.

According to Ptolemy, Lyra is like Venus and Mercury. It is said to give a harmonious, poetic and developed nature, fondness of music and aptness in science and art, but inclined to theft. It is associated by the Kabalists with the Hebrew letter Daleth and the fourth Tarot trump, 'The Emperor.'

Ophiuchus or Serpentarius: The Serpent Bearer (18N—24S)

This constellation is said to represent the infant Hercules, who strangled two serpents sent by Juno to kill him as he lay asleep in his cradle. (See Serpens.) For those who believe in a 14-sign zodiac, Ophiuchus is a zodiacal constellation.

Below: **The Horsehead Nebula in Orion (also see photo on page 104). The horsehead was not visible to the ancients.**

According to Ptolemy, it is like Saturn and moderately like Venus. It is said to give a passionate, blindly good-hearted, wasteful and easily seduced nature, together with little happiness, unseen dangers, enmity, strife and slander. Pliny said that it occasioned much mortality by poisoning. This constellation has also been called Aesculapius, and held to rule medicines. It is associated by the Kabalists with the Hebrew letter 'Ayin and the sixteenth Tarot trump, 'The Lightning-Struck Tower.'

Orion: The Giant, or Hunter (24N—13S)

The giant Orion was created out of an ox hide by the gods Jupiter, Neptune and Mercury, at the request of Hyreus, who had entertained them. He was blinded by Oenopion and Bacchus for his treatment of the former's daughter, but recovered his sight by exposing his eyes to the rising sun. In consequence of his boast that he could slay any beast bred upon the Earth, the scorpion (Scorpio) was brought forth, and Orion died from its sting.

According to Ptolemy, the bright stars—with the exception of Betelgeuze and Bellatrix—are like Jupiter and Saturn. It is said to give a strong and dignified nature, self-confidence, inconstancy, arrogance, violence, impiety, prosperity in trade—particularly by voyages or abroad—but also danger of treachery and poison. It was thought by the Romans to be very harmful to cattle and productive of storms. It is associated by the Kabalists with the Hebrew letter Aleph and the first Tarot trump, 'The Juggler.'

Pegasus: The Flying Horse (3N—36N)

Pegasus was born from the blood of Medusa after Perseus had cut off her head, and was afterwards tamed and ridden by Bellerophon. Being weary of earthly affairs, Bellerophon attempted to fly to heaven but fell off, and Pegasus continued his course, entered heaven and took his place among the stars.

According to Ptolemy, the bright stars are like Mars and Mercury. The constellation gives ambition, vanity, intuition, enthusiasm, caprice and bad judgment.

Perseus: The Champion (30N—62N)

Perseus, the son of Jupiter and Danae, was furnished with the sword, cap and wings of Mercury and the shield of Minerva. He killed the Medusa by cutting off her head and afterwards rescued, then married, Andromeda. On his return home he inadvertently killed his grandfather Acrisius and pined away through grief, whereupon Jupiter took pity on him and placed him among the stars.

According to Ptolemy, Perseus is like Jupiter and Saturn. It is said to give an intelligent, strong, bold and adventurous nature, but a tendency to lying. It is associated by the Kabalists with the Hebrew letter Lamed and the twelfth Tarot trump, 'The Hanged Man.'

Pisces: The Fishes (0N—32N)

Aphrodite and her son Eros (or in Roman mythology, Venus and Cupid), while sitting on the bank of the Euphrates, suddenly saw

Below left: The star cluster known as Trapezium, in the central region of the Orion Nebula. *Below:* A US Naval Observatory photo of the Spiral Galaxy in Pegasus, the flying horse. Pegasus is said to share qualities of Mars and Mercury to give ambition, intuition, vanity and bad judgement.

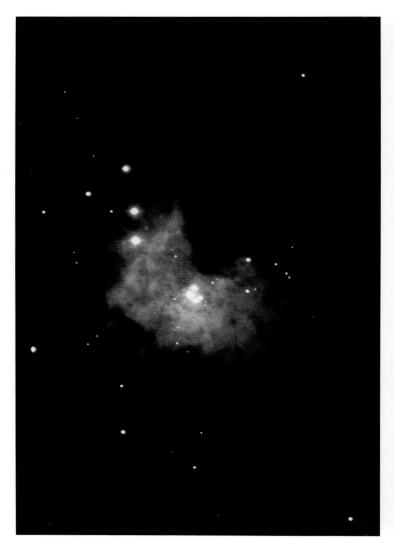

Typhon, the enemy of the gods, approaching them. They leapt into the river and were saved from drowning by two fishes, who were afterwards placed in the heavens by Venus in gratitude for their help. (See page 90.)

Ptolemy observes that, 'Those stars in Pisces which are in the head of the southern fish have the same influence as Mercury, and, in some degree, as Saturn; those in the body are like Jupiter and Mercury; those in the tail and in the southern line are like Saturn, and, moderately, like Mercury. In the northern fish, those stars on its body and backbone resemble Jupiter, and also Venus in some degree; those in the northern line are like Saturn and Jupiter.'

Pisces is associated by the Kabalists with the Hebrew letter Pe and the seventeenth Tarot trump, 'The Stars.'

Piscis Australis: The Southern Fish (28S—36S)

Pisces is not be confused with Piscis Australis, which is another of the 48 cardinal constellations. It is said to commemorate the transformation of Venus into the shape of a fish on one occasion while she was bathing.

Ptolemy gives no separate influence and only describes the star Fomalhaut, but according to Bayer, the constellation is of the nature of Saturn. It is said to have an influence similar to that of Pisces, but, in addition, to augment the fortunes.

Piscis Volans: The Flying Fish (63S—74S)

Neither Pisces or Piscis Australis should be confused with this constellation, which was added by Bayer in 1604. It is usually known as Volans, and is said to give a quick mind, activity, emotion, imagination and poetic or artistic ability.

Sagitta: The Arrow (15N—22N)

Sagitta represent the arrow with which Hercules slew the eagle that fed upon the liver of Prometheus.

According to Ptolemy, this constellation is like Saturn and moderately like Venus, but Bayer states that it is of the nature of Mars and Venus. It is said to give a keen mind with ability for abstract thought and teaching or writing, irritability, jealousy and danger of hostility and bodily harm.

Sagittarius: The Archer (20S—50S)

This constellation represents the wise and just Centaur Chiron, who was killed by accidentally dropping one of the poisoned arrows of Hercules upon his foot. (See page 78.)

The following are Ptolemy's remarks: 'The stars at the point of the arrow in Sagittarius have influence similar to that of Mars and the Moon; those on the bow, and at the grasp of the hand, act like Jupiter and Mars... Those in the waist and in the back resemble Jupiter, and also Mercury moderately; those in the feet, Jupiter and Saturn.'

By the Kabalists Sagittarius is associated with the Hebrew letter Vav and the sixth Tarot trump, 'The Lovers.'

Scorpio: The Scorpion (7S—46S)

This constellation represents the scorpion that killed Orion. (See Orion.)

Ptolemy observes that, 'The bright stars in the front of the body of Scorpio have an effect similar to that produced by the influence of Mars, and partly to that produced by Saturn; the three in the body itself... are similar to Mars and moderately to Jupiter; those in the joints of the tail are like Saturn and partly like Venus; those in the stinger, like Mercury and Mars.' (See page 74.)

Scorpio is associated by the Kabalists with the Hebrew letter 'Ayin and the sixteenth Tarot trump, 'The Lightning-Struck Tower.'

Serpens: The Serpent (26N—17S)

When Glaucus, son of Minos, the King of Crete, was drowned in a barrel of red honey, Aesculapius was sent for to restore him to life and was shut up in a secret chamber with the body. While he stood wondering what to do, a serpent entered, which he slew. Thereupon another serpent came in bearing a herb which it placed on the head of the dead serpent, thereby restoring it to life. Aesculapius, using the same herb, succeeded in restoring Glaucus. The serpent was placed in heaven, and for this reason certain writers have identified Ophiuchus with Aesculapius. According to other accounts the serpent is one of those that would have slain Hercules in his cradle. (See Ophiuchus.)

According to Ptolemy, Serpens is like Saturn and Mars. It is said to give wisdom, craft, deceit, malice, a feeble will and danger of poison.

Taurus: The Bull (34N—2S)

Jupiter, assuming the form of a bull, mingled with the herd when Europa, with whom he was infatuated, and her maidens disported themselves on the seashore. Encouraged by the tameness of the bull, Europa mounted it, where upon the god rushed into the sea and bore her away to Crete. According to other accounts Taurus represents Io, whom Jupiter turned into a cow in order to deceive Juno. (See page 50.)

Ptolemy observes that, 'Those stars in Taurus which are in the abscission of the sign resemble in their temperament the influence of Venus, and in some degree that of Saturn... The stars in the head (except Alderbaran) resemble Saturn, and, partly, Mercury; and those at the top of the horns are like Mars.'

Taurus is associated by the Kabalists with the Hebrew letter Aleph and the first Tarot trump, 'The Juggler.' In all the ancient zodiacs, Taurus is the beginning sign and marked the Vernal Equinox from about 4000 to 1700 BC.

Taurus is not to be confused with Taurus Poniatovii (Pon-

At left: **The Trifid ('three-lobed') Nebula in Sagittarius, the archer. Representing the mythic centaur Chiron, this constellation has an extraordinary number of attributable effects (see text).** *At right:* **The Spiral Galaxy in the constellation Triangulum, the benevolent triangle.**

iatowski's Bull), located at 11N—5S, which was formed by the Abbé Poczobut of Wilna in honor of Stanislaus Poniatowski, the King of Poland. It is said to give obstinacy and changeability, emotion, honor and renown.

Triangulum: The Triangle (30N—37N)

Triangulum is said to have been placed in the heavens by Jupiter at the request of Ceres, who asked that the shape of her beloved island of Sicily might be represented amongst the stars.

According to Ptolemy, it is like Mercury, said to give a just, companionable, truthful, righteous and benevolent nature, with interest in architecture and Freemasonry.

Triangulum should not be confused with Triangulum Minor (The Lesser Triangle), located at 28N—33N, formed by Hevelius in 1690, or Triangulum Australe (The Southern Triangle), located at 61S—71S, which is attributed to Pieter Theodor of the sixteenth century, although both of these constellations have an influence that is similar to that of Triangulum.

Ursa Major: The Great Bear, or Big Dipper (33N—73N)

Callisto, daughter of Lycaon, the King of Arcadia, of whom Jupiter was enamored, became a follower of Diana due to her love of hunting. Jupiter sought Callisto by assuming the form of Diana, and Juno, who discovered the intrigue, turned Callisto into a bear. Angry that the bear was placed in heaven, Juno requested her brother Neptune never to let those stars set within his kingdom, and for this reason they are always above the horizon in Europe. To account for the length of the bear's tail, it is said that Jupiter, fearing her teeth, lifted her by the tail, which became stretched because of her weight and the distance from Earth to heaven.

According to Ptolemy, Ursa Major is like Mars. It is said to give a quiet, prudent, suspicious, mistrustful, self-controlled, patient nature, but also an uneasy spirit and great anger and revengefulness when roused. It is associated by the Kabalists with the Hebrew letter Zayin and the seventh Tarot trump, 'The Chariot.'

Ursa Minor: The Little Bear, or Little Dipper (69N—90N)

According to some accounts this constellation represents Arcas, son of Callisto and Jupiter. (See Bootes and Ursa Major.) Other writers state that it is meant to represent Cynosura, one of the Nymphs of Crete who reared the infant Jupiter—the other, Helice, being Ursa Major.

According to Ptolemy, the bright stars are like Saturn and in some degree like Venus. It is said to give indifference and improvidence of spirit, and to lead to many troubles. It is associated by the Kabalists with the Hebrew letter Tav and the twenty-first Tarot trump, 'The Universe.'

Virgo: The Virgin (16N—15S)

This constellation is said to represent Justitia, daughter of Astraeus and Ancora, although other accounts speak of Erigone, daughter of Icarius, who hanged herself through grief at the death of her father. (See Bootes.) Ptolemy observes that, 'The stars in the head of Virgo, and that at the top of the southern wing, operate like Mercury and somewhat like Mars; the other bright stars in the same wing, and those about the girdle, resemble Mercury in their influence, and also Venus, moderately… Those at the points of the feet and at the bottom of the garments are like Mercury, and also Mars, moderately.' (See page 66.)

It is associated by the Kabalists with the Hebrew letter Gimel and the third Tarot trump, 'The Empress.'

At right: **The Eagle Nebula in Serpens, the serpent. The Serpent is said to impart the mixed qualities of wisdom, craftiness, and danger of poison.**

INDEX

PICTURE CREDITS

American Graphic Systems Archives 1, 3, 4-5, 7, 9, 10 (bottom left), 11, 12 (all), 13, 14 (all), 15 (top left, right), 17 (all), 21, 22, 23, 24 (all), 36, 37, 39, 46 (top), 47 (right), 50, 51 (bottom left, right), 54 (top), 55 (bottom right), 58 (top), 59 (bottom left), 62 (top), 66 (top), 70 (top), 74 (top), 78 (all), 80 (all), 82 (top), 83 (bottom left), 86 (top), 88 (top center), 90 (top), 95, 105, 121, 122, 127, 128
BBC Hulton Picture Library 57 (top)
Chateau Versailles 64 (top left), 75 (bottom left)
Cinema Collectors 46 (bottom), 48 (top left, right), 49, 52 (all), 54 (bottom), 56 (top right, bottom), 58 (bottom), 59 (bottom right), 61, 62 (bottom), 64 (top right), 65, 66 (bot-

tom), 67 (bottom left, right), 68 (top left, center), 69, 72 (top right, bottom), 73, 75 (bottom right), 77, 81, 85, 86 (bottom), 87 (bottom left, right), 88 (top left, bottom), 92 (all)
Cinema Shop 47 (left), 63 (bottom right), 71 (bottom left, right), 79 (bottom left), 90 (bottom), 91 (bottom right)
©Lee Coombs 2-3, 40-41, 42-43, 44-45, 104, 111, 112
Hale Observatories 6, 40
Robert Hunt Picture Library 88 (top right)
Anwar Hussein 72 (top left), 76 (top right)
Illustrated London News Picture Library 60 (top right)
Martin Luther King Jr Center For Non-violent Social Change 82 (top right)
Kitt Peak National Observatory 38,

116-117
Lorimar Productions 68 (top right)
©Reverend MJ McPike Collection 10 (top), 23, 25, 26 (both), 28, 29, 30, 32, 33, 34-35
NASA 31, 55 (bottom left), 97, 98, 99, 100, 101, 102, 106, 107, 114
National Baseball Hall of Fame and Museum Inc 79 (bottom right)
National Gallery of Art 91 (bottom left)
National Portrait Gallery, London 57 (bottom left)
New Zealand High Commission, London 60 (top left)
Nixon Presidential Materials Project 84
Photoresources 27
S&G Press Agency 53
Smithsonian Institution 10 (bottom center, right)

South Dakota Department of Tourism 94
Sun Entertainment Corp 72 (top center)
TASS via Sovfoto 48 (bottom)
US Naval Observatory 42, 44, 108-109, 113 (all), 115
Universal City Studios 57 (bottom center)
The White House 56 (top left), 70 (bottom)
Michael Evans 19, 89
©Bill Yenne 8, 15 (bottom), 47 (top), 51 (top), 55 (top), 57 (bottom left), 59 (top), 63 (top, bottom left), 67 (top), 70 (top), 71 (top), 75 (top), 79 (top), 83 (top, bottom right), 87 (top), 91 (top), 96, 123 (all), 124 (all), 125 (all), 126 (all)

Designed by Bill Yenne; Captioned by Timothy Jacobs

The 12 signs of the Zodiac are displayed across the gatefold which follows, starting from the left with Pisces, the fish (February 19–March 21), all the way back through the year to Aries, the ram (March 21–April 20). The signs are presented here as they follow the plane of the ecliptic (the Sun's path through the sky), and in their relation to other familiar constellations.

Surrounding the Zodiac can also be seen Andromeda, the seated woman; Aquila, the eagle; Lyra, the lyre; Bootes, the plowman; Serpens, the serpent; Orion, the hunter; and others—including two halves of Cetus, the whale (shown here at left and right, to represent the continuity of the year-round cycle).